GOODBYE BRITAIN

Talking to the Brits Who Packed Their Bags and Left

TOM BECK

First published by Keep Your Composure in 2021

ISBN: 978-1-8384076-0-5

The names of some of the individuals featured in this book have been changed to protect their privacy.
Please don't be weird and try finding them.

For more information about this book:
GoodbyeBritain.co.uk

Cover Design: Sophie Lauren Smith
You can see more of her awesome work on Instagram:
@Sketch.The.Adventure

CONTENTS

Contents

Contents

The words featured in this book were
spoken between March and August 2020.

MAKING THE MOVE

TOM – GERMANY

Sitting at my desk one day, in a quiet corner of an out-of-town business park in Berkshire, it dawned on me that I was the odd one out in my department. With a South African in front of me, an Indian to my right, and a Pakistani colleague opposite him, I was the only person still living in their home country. And it didn't end there, either. Within my wider team, I worked alongside a Polish guy who ran a Chinese restaurant on the side, his Mauritian teammate, a Honduran software developer who eventually moved to Spain, a Ukrainian account manager, and a Russian assistant. While there were a handful of other British people in the building, I'd regularly meet Germans, Italians, French, and Romanian colleagues while queuing for lunch, too. I'm sure you get the picture by now. Considering this was in the average British town, in a fairly run of the mill corporate job, the cultural diversity was impressive. And there I was, working a short drive from where I'd spent the best part of the last thirty years.

While the idea of emigrating had always appealed, I'd never

felt a pressing need to act on it. I was living happily on the tube map, enjoyed having friends and family close by, and loved that my football team were on my doorstep. Though I'd studied up north in Manchester, during which I spent a summer teaching American kids to climb trees in Pennsylvania, most of my life had played out at different stops along the Metropolitan line. I'd lived in Chalfont, gone to school in Chesham, moved to Chorleywood, then Ruislip, and eventually to Northwood, and worked in various parts of central London. Being close enough to the city, but far enough away to have a garden and a parking space, meant that I had the best of both worlds in my mind. The capital city has always inspired me and given me a great deal of energy, too. I think Craig Taylor in his excellent book "Londoners", from which I've drawn undeniable influence, captured my thoughts perfectly when he described the city as having great 'propulsion'. As a collection of people, places, and attitudes, the city is a driving force, and certainly one that pushes me forward whenever I'm there. Sure, it can also be relentlessly tiring, but I've always wanted to be tired from my own actions, rather than well rested from the things I've haven't done.

So, if I was enjoying life in London so much, why do I now find myself as an immigrant in what was formerly East Germany? Let me explain. A few years prior to making the move, I was unexpectedly offered a good career opportunity with a global company. The office was based an hour outside of the city unfortunately, but the salary and benefits softened that blow considerably. Taking the job initially seemed like a great idea, but daily life there felt increasingly stale once I'd settled in. It soon became apparent that I'd swapped an exciting role in a youthful, but unpredictable start-up, for a steady job at a slower paced corporate company that was flooded with middle managers. I'd also gone from wandering along the South Bank on my lunchbreak, to walking through a housing estate on my own to buy a drink from the local Post Office. To be fair to the recruitment consultant, I did have the good salary, the car allowance, and the health insurance that he'd promised me, so it wasn't all bad. I knew I was fortunate to be in that position, especially when looking back at my former roles in London, so I committed to the idea for as long as I could. That was until Britain decided to leave the European Union, however.

On the drive to the office one February morning, they interrupted the radio show to announce that a referendum was to be held in the summer. I wasn't initially concerned, believing that the idea seemed farfetched and irrational, but that made the subsequent result far harder to swallow. Without wanting to go into the wider politics, as others can articulate their thoughts on that more eloquently than I ever could, I strongly disagreed with the decision. While the impact on trade and the economy was a worry, the idea that British citizens would lose our rights to freely live and work in twenty-seven other European nations was a real blow. Working in that office once the votes were counted, surrounded by people who'd improved their own lives through emigration, made me realise that I had to try that for myself. I wanted to see what it was like to step away from your own country and start a new life elsewhere. Of course, there were no guarantees that I'd enjoy the experience, but I was willing to take that risk. And so that decision, which millions of my compatriots voted in favour of, started a countdown in my head. I knew I could either continue working in that business park while the window to the rest of Europe closed in front of me, or I could jump through it and see where I landed. It wasn't quite now or never, given the complex negotiations that lay ahead, but I didn't want that window to slam shut in front of me, either. So as the dust settled on the referendum results, I told my boss that I wanted to move, started looking for opportunities, and eventually found an internal role in Potsdam. I said goodbye to Britain in September 2017 and haven't looked back since.

Goodbye Britain

My second working day in Germany landed on my birthday and, though I'd mentioned it to my new team the day before, not one single person remembered it. It's not that I was expecting a big fuss, I just didn't think it would be completely ignored, either. As I'd moved across on my own, with my wife joining a fortnight later, it made for a lonely few day in my new home. It took until the next team birthday, when the guy celebrating it booked a meeting in which he offered everyone a slice of *bienenstich* (bee sting cake), for me to understand why my own birthday was ignored. The idea that you bring the cake to share with others on your special day, and with a formal meeting invite too, is something I've grown to accept about life here. And by that, I do mean begrudgingly accept, as I still refuse to book a meeting for my own birthday. But it's those small cultural differences, and I've found hundreds over the last few years, which have caught me out here at times.

Despite the inauspicious start, settling into Germany was relatively straightforward. With the help of a relocation agent, I quickly found an apartment, registered as a resident, and was guided through the mountain of federal bureaucracy with just a few signatures. Having an agent was a surreal experience, especially as my own regularly referred to me as 'Mr President' whenever introducing me to a landlord or utilities company. It felt like I was a celebrity for a week, one that was driven around town and simply had to sign paperwork when the time was right. That support soon dropped off, after which I didn't see or hear from my agent again. It made the transition a fun experience though, rather than anything too stressful.

Having only seen Potsdam briefly before moving here, it's proven to be a fantastic place to live. We're surrounded by lakes and rivers and are spoilt for choice with our palaces, parks, and monuments. We've then got leading universities, extensive research facilities, and the world's oldest large-scale film studios here. It's an area of the country that's rich in history, too. It was previously the summer home of both a Prussian King, Frederick the Great, and the Nobel Prize winning physicist Albert Einstein. And to this day, you can see their influence in the city's architecture, its' investment in science, and the naming of several local coffee shops, too. The city was also the scene for several pivotal moments in world history. The Potsdam Conference of 1945 saw Churchill, Stalin, and Truman meet at Schloss Cecilienhof to decide how to govern post-war Germany. Then a short walk along the river from there is Glienicker Brücke, more commonly known as the Bridge of Spies. This was a check point between West and East Germany during the Cold War, with Potsdam located in the latter, that was occasionally used to strategically trade captured spies between America and the Soviet Union. The area has moved on considerably since then, but they've respectfully maintained these locations so future generations can learn from them. The modern city is also not without its flaws, its excessive drive to replace park land with apartment blocks for example, but they obviously pale in comparison to what's gone before them. Further afield, we've also got the sights and sounds of Berlin just a short train ride away when we need them.

Now, the irony of moving abroad because I felt like the odd one out in my own country, is that I'm often the odd one out here, too. Obviously, when relocating to Germany, I expected to be surrounded by Germans. What took me by surprise here, is that many of my neighbours still identify as East German first and foremost. Though the Berlin Wall fell in 1989, with the country being reunified the following year, there are still several generations worth of lifestyles, behaviours, and attitudes left standing in the East. The locals here are rightly proud of their heritage and admirably resist attempts to gentrify where they live, but it does often feel like the area is playing catch up with the rest of the country. In fact, you still hear people unkindly refer to this area as *Dunkeldeutschland*, a nickname given to East Germany due to its historic lack of streetlights. With many international citizens opting to live over the state border in Berlin, English speaking residents, whether natively or not, are relatively rare. And having lived under Soviet rule for long periods, with Russian being their foreign language of choice, some of the older residents have had very little exposure to foreigners. It can make you feel unwelcomed in some situations, as trying to play for a local football team proved, but fortunately those incidents are few and far between. On the flip side, I've never seen so many men with mullets wearing double-denim before in my life.

In general, emigrating to Germany has been a fantastic experience so far and one that's given me far more confidence. You regularly hear the phrase 'take yourself out of your comfort zone', and life here regularly forces me to do just that. With speaking a new language and adapting to a different culture, everyday activities such as going to the dentist or simply asking for help in a shop can seem like daunting prospects in German. Yet getting through them, no matter how small they seem on the surface, brings with it a real sense of accomplishment. It doesn't always go smoothly, and there have been times when I've felt deeply embarrassed or incredibly frustrated, but these experiences all add up.

When you speak to British people about living in Germany, regardless of which generation you talk to, you'll often hear the same three topics time and time again. That's if you ignore misguided attempts to reference the war, of course. The idea that Germans are inherently efficient is often a talking point, especially when compared to the shambles with which we perceive our own country to be in. While trains can run on time here, I've also experienced long delays and will gasp at some of the prices they charge for longer journeys. And as anyone who has dealt with their local Rathaus can attest to, the bureaucracy here can be cripplingly slow and illogical at times. The second topic is the belief that Germans have no sense of humour, which is plainly not the case. The difference is that their sense of humour is often very literal or matter of fact, as opposed to our very dry and sarcastic quips in the UK. For me, someone who finds great pleasure in a quick-witted response, I routinely forget that my jokes will be taken at face value. In fact, sometimes my life can feel like the most painful stand-up comedy routine of all time, as I often need to explain the nuances of my humour to perplexed locals. Then finally, many think that that living in Germany is just one long Oktoberfest, which, as you've probably guessed, is also not the case. While Oktoberfest, a folk festival celebrated each September in Munich, is popular, it happens over three hundred and fifty miles away from where I live. I can drink beer and eat pretzels if I want to, but it's not part of everyday life here. My diet also doesn't predominantly consist of bratwurst, as much as my Dad would like to believe.

I poke fun at my adopted country, but I am eternally grateful for the opportunities here and the lifestyle it affords me. Germany is a well-run and much respected country and one that I intend to build my future around. And those points aren't indirect criticisms of the UK, as I honestly hold no resentment or ill-feelings there. I can miss elements of my former life, but I've also never been someone who suffers from homesickness or has a deep longing to return to former times. It's more that I've found a new home here that works for me, and I'm hoping that continues for the foreseeable future.

Over the last fifty years, millions of other Brits have opted for life outside the British Isles, too. And according to the latest statistics, just under one million of those can also currently be found in EU member countries. In terms of popularity though, our desired destinations are still those where English is the native language, with the United States, Canada, Australia, and New Zealand topping the list. With such high numbers, I've always known that my own emigration story is far from unique or particularly interesting. And that same sentiment applies to many of us that live or have lived abroad, I'm sure. For every family renovating a chateau in France, late night talk show host in America, or newfound lemon farmers in Tuscany, there are thousands of Brits living everyday lives across the world. Their stories may not be worth drawn-out dramatizations or bestselling books on their own, but as a group they offer fascinating insights into modern British emigration. So that's exactly what I set out to do. To speak to British people from a range of backgrounds, who packed their bags, said goodbye to Britain, and moved their lives to different countries across the world.

What started with me catching up with British friends in other countries, quickly became a search to find others willing to talk to me. I posted in 'ex-pat' groups, browsed hashtags, and asked for personal introductions to other likeminded immigrants. That led to over one hundred spoken conversations with British people across the globe, many of whom were strangers that simply trusted in my idea. The calls were at all times of the day and night, lasted anywhere from twenty minutes to three hours, and, naturally, all began with small talk about the weather. I connected with people in thirty-nine different countries, phoned six different continents, and spent over five thousand minutes hearing their personal stories.

What I always found interesting about my former foreign colleagues, was how their lives had led them to that business park in Berkshire. Why did they initially leave their country behind and try living somewhere else? Over time, I discovered that some had emigrated as children, others had moved for work or new opportunities, a few had fallen in love and followed their hearts, and several simply wanted to experience life beyond their own borders. And it was those same reasons that many of the people featured in this book gave when I spoke to them, too.

When meeting these Brits, either face to face, on a video link, or through an old-fashioned phone call, the first question I'd always ask them was 'Why?' And that relatively opened ended question led to some great conversations with a wide mix of personalities. Rarely did any of their stories or anecdotes neatly fit into just one category, however. I met people who moved for work but found love. I heard from those who chased their dreams and ended up dealing with crushing disappointment. And I also spoke to folk who had enjoyed their experiences but were happy to return to the UK at the end of it. I listened to adventurous tales, empathised with personal tragedies, related to the elation and fears of failure, and laughed at the sarcastic responses.

The following chapters contain edited extracts from the conversations I had with people who said goodbye to Britain. They represent the spoken thoughts of those featured and capture their opinions and feelings at that point in time. I'm grateful to everyone who let me into their lives and has since trusted me with their words; I hope I've done them justice here.

SEEKING ADVENTURES

PAUL – ARGENTINA

I was born in Manchester and lived in an area synonymous with drug dealers and violence. To avoid that, we were sent to a better school that was three different bus rides away. That was back when you had absolutely nothing to do on a bus, too. There were no mobile phones or music, so it was fucking dull at times, mate. In many ways, I'd already grown sick of commuting early on. After university, where I studied economics in Newcastle, I took myself off down to London like I was Dick fucking Whittington. I ended up doing some well-paid accounting jobs for several big companies, these decent roles that I was supposed to be excited about. Earning big money is always nice, isn't it?

In my private life at the time, I'd got married to someone too soon and it didn't work out. We eventually broke up and got divorced. It happens, but it meant my social scene dried up and I didn't really have any mates to fall back on. It really hit me hard, that, and definitely changed my mentality in a lot of ways. I started looking at new jobs, too, just something that I can get my teeth into, take my mind off it, and really believe in it all again. I looked at all these highly paid jobs at big brands, just because I knew I could land one of them. I went for an interview at one, and there's this offer on the table, huge money really, and the guy asks me how I feel about it. I just looked at him, held my hands up, and said, 'I'm trying to work out how I'd motivate myself to turn up here every day.' It was raw, brutal honesty from me. He appreciated that, but was blunt back and said, 'Sounds like you should sort your shit out, Paul,' and he was totally right.

I continued looking for roles though and thought I'd found this ideal one, working for an ethical company in South London. Their website said everything you wanted to hear. Their package and offer were great and all that. I'd even started looking at houses in that area, just so I didn't have to bloody commute. Then just when I thought that job offer was coming, the rug got pulled from under me and they went with an internal candidate. I was fucking gutted, to be honest. I just sat there and thought, 'What the fuck am I going to do now?' I was in a rut and not particularly enjoying life in London anymore, so I knew I needed to find something else. At first, I considered taking my interest in maths and statistics, things like that, and becoming a teacher. However, my friend's parents were always very Labour leaning back in the day, so the idea of teaching in England was beaten the fuck out of us growing up in Thatcher's Britain. They'd seen public services being slashed, so were naturally against anything like that. Thinking back to that, all the times I'd listened to them, I soon knocked that idea on its head.

The thought of making a career change and possibly into teaching, that didn't really go away, though. And it was actually a present my ex-wife gave, a holiday to Buenos Aires, that sparked something. We'd been out there, absolutely loved it, and it made me think I could go back over there, teach some English, and just see what it was like living there. I quit my job in the October, served my notice, and moved out to Argentina in the January.

Before going, I'd researched absolutely everything I could online. Where to live, what to do, who to speak to, absolutely everything. I felt as ready as I could ever be, but I'd be lying if I said I knew exactly how it would all pan out.

I couldn't speak more than a few words of Spanish when I arrived, so I was trying to do things like get a mobile phone and that was a fucking nightmare. I was sold a dodgy sim card and the phone wouldn't work, so not a great start. I also had a nightmare with places I was staying. One of the first places I went, it was just absolutely filthy. It was a disgusting place, mate, it smelled awful. I was also the only forty something year old staying with these twenty somethings, these little oiks that didn't clean up after themselves. Then at another place, I was staying with this older woman who'd just completely lost the plot. She's screaming at me in Spanish, accusing me of trying to touch her up. And there's me, I'm just getting some cereal in the kitchen, minding my own business. It was really full on at times, and quite a chaotic introduction to the country.

You know, it took me a while to realise that I couldn't just use my old London tactics and expect it all to work in Argentina. Back in London, I could just complain to someone, go there and sort it out, or just argue back and let them have it. Here? That wouldn't work. I just thought to myself, 'Why am I dealing with this shit?' I knew I wasn't going back though, admitting that I've failed there because of a few rough days? No chance. Failure meant going back, putting that corporate tie around my neck, and fucking commuting. I've already told you how much I fucking hated commuting, haven't I? Instead of putting up with it, I just grabbed all my stuff, banged on my laptop, and just found a new place to fucking stay. It was that realisation that I was putting up with all this shit for nothing, that gave me a real sense of freedom. Once I dropped that weight off my shoulders, decided to take no more bullshit from people, I really kicked on and haven't looked back.

Argentina has been a blast, mate. The people here, they often
have no filter at all, which makes for an interesting time. You'll
be teaching someone English, and they just lay everything on the
table, right there in front of you. They're talking about illness,
they're talking about their sex life, they're giving intimate,
graphic, sometimes disgusting information. There just aren't
any barriers. It blew my mind at first, being English and all, but
I really bought into the whole style. Sometimes that approach,
it can come across a little crazy, but you settle into it. You'll
also hear people say that the Argentine women are mad, a bit
dramatic, too much effort. To be honest, I've never found that.
Perhaps it's because I'm meeting the older ones these days,
but they've all been great. I've met some absolutely gorgeous
women out here, mate, absolutely gorgeous. In fact, I've met this
incredible woman here, a really fantastic Argentine lady. We
have a great time, we're always making plans, always coming up
with travel ideas. I'm really happy with her.

I'm sure if people from London see me now, they'll think that
I'm just scruffy git that's earning about three percent of what
I could. I just don't care. I feel free here, more like I can enjoy
myself. I felt like I needed to reinvent my life, to change it all,
to have a bit of a crazy time. Have I had that? Absolutely. Do I
regret any of it? Absolutely fucking not.

MAT – FINLAND, AUSTRALIA, CHINA, & SPAIN

It's very hard to get out of Fishguard. It's in the middle of
nowhere, out on the coast, and only around five thousand people
live there. The ferry goes from Fishguard over to the island twice
a day. If it wasn't for that ferry and the nature, that place would
just disappear. I was desperate to get out of there, really. I really
wanted to get out of Wales, to travel, to have some adventure.
The real world feels like something you see on television when

you live there, it does.

When I first got out, my father was living in the south of Spain and I went out on a whim to see him. I wasn't there long. I ended up meeting my cousin and his friend, and said I'd join them as they sailed this boat down to the south of France. I jumped on in Malaga with them, sailed for twenty-eight days, and then jumped off in Nice. I wasn't really sure what to do, then. I was free of Fishguard, which was the main thing, and I just felt like I suddenly had the world in front of me. Anyway, I got off the boat that morning and thought I'd head back towards Malaga on the train and work it all out. I got on, looked for an attractive looking woman, I'll be honest, and sat near her. I ended up talking to this French girl for a while, then a Mexican guy got talking to her, and the three of us then decided we'd head to Barcelona, just like that. That just felt like a great plan at the time, just going with these spur of the moment ideas as I went.

There's a lot of illegal hostels in Barcelona. You get these travellers who work for them and they'll just be out on Las Ramblas picking up people who had nowhere else to stay. Me and this French girl, we turned out to be two of those people getting picked up. This Australian girl spotted us, explained that the hostel didn't have an official name and all that, and took us to this six-floor building that was just full of bunkbeds. You just came and went when you wanted and there was no real security in there. We walked in and I met my future wife in the lobby, there and then. It went from there, basically. At that point, I stayed in Spain, but I came to Finland twice and tried to live here, but both times I didn't like it. I don't think I was ready. I was in my mid-twenties and I was still in party mode. I ended up running one of the illegal hostels for a year, instead. I would end up going back out to Las Ramblas every night, picking up backpackers and bringing them in.

It got a little crazy from there, really. I eventually followed my future wife to China, blagged some English teaching out there, got married to her in Australia and spent a year there. Then we went traveling in South East Asia, Japan, India, spent some time in Central America. It was a bit mad. We didn't know where we wanted to settle for a few years, so just kept traveling and exploring new places. In among all that, it made sense for me to call Finland my home as it were, so I moved there for the third and, what seems to be, final time. The travel bug had died down by then and I'd grown a little tired of it all, really. I figured I'd give that up, learn Finnish as best I could, and finally settle down in one place.

It's a really tough nut to crack Finland, it is. No matter what qualifications you have, unless you work in IT or you're a scientist, then you're pretty much starting from the bottom if you don't speak Finnish. Myself, I had to do all these crap jobs when I came here. I was collecting glasses in a nightclub surrounded by teenagers at first. I then washed dishes. I did some waitering. I worked as a human donkey during conferences. It's definitely a bit of a slog if you're foreign at times, and you do have to work harder than any of the Finnish people to prove yourself. That's just what it takes, though. I took the opportunity to learn Finnish while working these jobs. I put a load of effort in, I'd take lessons, listen to audio books, use apps, and even then, it's still very hard. It's hard to speak it, but also hard to understand people. That's why there's a lot of animosity in general, I think. Most people seem to meet a Finnish woman, move here, expect the country to adapt to them and not the other way round, and then really struggle. The Finnish aren't the easiest at times, either. They're quite introvert, so they don't really do small talk with people. You've got foreigners coming here, it doesn't work out for them, it doesn't work out in their marriage, and they're just left with bitterness and resentment. You'll see the same thing happen all the time, and they'll often take to the internet to vent about it, too.

For me, I'm now back in college again, at the age of forty-one, getting my plumbing papers here. I should have them by December, I think. Then I'll be a qualified plumber here, speaking Finnish, earning a decent enough wage. It's a respected profession here, too. I'll be happy fitting bathrooms, fixing radiators, making some money, and then just going home. It'll finally work for me, that.

DAVID - SOUTH KOREA

I'd meet people who'd lived on a Kibbutz in Israel, or who'd spent three months in South Africa, and I'd be like, 'Well, I've been to Euro Disney.' I just didn't have the same experiences, but it made me want to travel or live somewhere else after university. I also wanted to find an experience that no-one else had told me about. I didn't want to replicate anything, even if someone else's experience had sounded fun. I took a four-week teaching English as a foreign language course, signed up with an agency, and moved to South Korea shortly after.

The agent told me that I was moving to this thriving ex-pat community, that it was close to the beaches, the mountains, and a short train ride to Seoul. That all sounded great, but I didn't really want a thriving ex-pat community, if I was honest. At the same time, I didn't want to be stuck by myself in some backwater town, completely unable to relate to anyone I met. Anyway, when I got there, that thriving community turned out to be two Irish guys and a woman from New Zealand, and she was thirty-seven at the time. We used to joke that she was great, but she was old. It's funny, I'm thirty-eight now and I'm constantly telling myself that I'm not too old. The thing with the Irish guys was that they worked for a rival academy and I was explicitly told by my private academy not to talk to them. I had no other choice though. It felt like no one else in the whole town spoke English, so we inevitably became close and realized it wasn't an issue after all.

Now in South Korea, the drive for education is insane. Mostly in a good way, but they really, really, really value education. So, their kids go to school after school. They go to these academies after their regular schooling and everyone goes to at least the English academies, which was one of the places I was working. However, when the kids are super young they can go to things like magic academies, where you learn tricks, you can go to a music academy and learn an instrument, or you can do martial arts. Once they're older, they're then just really focused on exams, and they'll drop out of some of the more fun activities. Instead, they go to places that we'd call cram academies, where they cram as much information as possible in so they can pass their exams and get results.

I worked in that first private academy for a year, and during that year I met my wife. That was a big reason for me to stay in the country, too. I relocated to Seoul after that year, and that's a very different world. I think you can realistically say that in Korea you have Seoul and then the rest of Korea. It's a completely different experience there. I taught English for another year once I got to the city but stopped after that. I really enjoyed teaching itself, but I hated everything that came with it. The owners of these academies were naturally running them like businesses, and I get that, but it would often come at a cost to the actual learning. We'd have kids pushed into classes where the level was much higher than they could handle, but it was the only class they could attend that day and the owner didn't want to miss out. It just disrupted everything and would bring down the more advanced students. It ended up being this constant balance between the children's needs, the parents' expectations, and the business the whole time. If a child wasn't then quoting Shakespeare within four weeks, the parents would start asking questions. Eventually, I just had enough of doing that and found a job outside of teaching.

The way society functions in South Korea is based around your age. If you were a year older than me, I'd talk to you very differently to how I would if you were a year younger. The Koreans understand that foreigners don't necessarily know these idiosyncrasies though, but they do end up affecting you. A team that I worked on, there were ten people. We had seven Koreans and three foreigners, of which I was the eldest of the foreigners. The way that the seating works, is that the team leader is the eldest person and he, and it is usually is he, sits closest to the window. The youngest person, they sit closest to the door or near where the elevator is. It then goes up in age. There was one point that the younger guy next to me was re-assigned and his replacement was then older than me, so I had to swap seats so he could sit closer to the window. I remember thinking it was utter lunacy. It doesn't really matter, but still the idea that you had to move based on your age was crazy. It does make you feel better about getting older, though, that's for sure.

There's also a very clear corporate ladder in companies in South Korea, and it's really, really automated. You'll go through the levels as you get older, so you'll start as a *sawon*, which is an employee, then you'll be a *daeri*, which is an assistant manager, and so on. It's very strict, and these ladders will often be the same regardless of the company or department you work for. One hugely positive thing about that, is that there's a lot less office politics or cutthroat behaviour. It still exists, but there's this belief that there's a system and a ladder to climb, and that you'll naturally climb it if you follow that system. What it means, is that people do what they're told. If their boss tells you what to do, you'll do it. If you have a good boss, that system works well. That dictator style system works well when you have a good dictator, it's a disaster if you don't, though.

I was in South Korea for nine years and I probably stayed there for three years too long. It was a fantastic experience, and I do miss it a lot, but I was always aware that I was different.

You get looked at when you go down the street, and you feel like you're in a fishbowl. In terms of a career, you can enter a company higher as a foreigner, but you'll rarely go anywhere from there. You'll be useful and you'll have a job, but you couldn't fully progress your career in the South Korea.

Having lived in several countries now, and we're currently in Barcelona, home is where my wife and my dog are. That's home for me. I'll always be English, and if anything, I feel more aware that I'm English now that I've left the country, but after five or six days of being back there, I'm glad I'm able to leave again.

TOM – COLOMBIA, NEW ZEALAND, & EL SALVADOR

When I was twenty-four, I quit my job, got rid of all my phone contacts, and booked a one-way flight to New Zealand via Central and South America. I was pretty disheartened with the UK by that point, to be honest. I'd fallen in with the wrong crowd, was probably drinking too much and taking too many recreational drugs, and I was just really unhappy with myself. I remember telling my Mum that I might never come back, and I think it broke her heart a little. She was worried about the way my life was going at the time, and she probably thought she'd never see me again. There was a chance of that, too, but at least that's not how it's ultimately worked out for me.

My life changed when I hit Mexico, really. I was traveling on my own for a start, and it just really allowed me to be myself for the first time in my life. I was experiencing these spiritually and energetically connected places, seeing such beautiful surroundings, and forming these great friendships with people I'd regularly meet on the trail. During the trip, I'd stop in places and do some volunteer work, too. Once of those places was in El Salvador, where I spent four months teaching English in the morning and helping to construct a school in the afternoon. It was crazy, to be honest. Some of the kids were in gangs, there'd be disease and rubbish everywhere, and we'd regularly see dead bodies by the side of the road. It was definitely an eye-opening experience, but a really worthy one, too. It also taught me that I could make a difference to people's lives, rather than just wasting my own back in Scotland.

It was on that trip, that the idea of going to Colombia was first planted in my head. I'd met up with a group of people in Panama and they were going to a New Year's Eve party in Santa Marta, Colombia. Back then, that area was this exotic, slightly dangerous, wild place that you'd read about in books but never dared to go yourself. I think seven people had been kidnapped in that area that year, too. So, when I told my father that I was thinking of going, he said he'd disown me if I did. I ended up listening for a change, and going down to Peru and Bolivia instead, but it really planted a seed in my mind. You know what it's like when someone tells you not to do something, it makes you really want to do it. So, it was always on my mind to go to Colombia and see it for myself.

I did make it onto New Zealand after that and worked for an airline up in Nelson for a year, before taking the slow route back to Scotland once my working holiday visa expired. Coming back to the UK after all that time away, that was one of the hardest things I've ever done. I've done it three times now and it doesn't get any easier. That entry back into the British orbit, it's mentally, financially, and emotionally a very tough time for me. It didn't help that I returned to the Isle of Skye, where my parents were running a restaurant at the time. It's a beautiful place, but the weather can be horrific, it can be cold and dark for long periods, and you can feel incredibly remote. I moved away eventually, landed a job for a big IT company in London, and bought a house in Brixton with some friends. It helped me build up a bit of experience and make some money while I was at it. I'll always credit that first trip away with giving me the confidence and the change of mindset to make all that possible, though.

Anyway, fast forward to 2010, when I finally got to Colombia for the first time. I went there for a three-week holiday with my brother and it was absolutely stunning. We went to Santa Marta, which wasn't quite as dangerous then, and I just fell in love with the place. I knew I wanted to find a way back to the country from that. I just had this burning desire to get out of the corporate chains that I found myself in, and instead follow something I could be passionate about. I didn't really have a particular plan in mind, but I just knew I had to try something. The following year, after meeting some friends in Panama and doing the San Blas Islands hopping trip, I landed back in Colombia again and this time, I stuck around.

I arrived in Medellín first and spent almost two months around that area, did a lot of Spanish tuition, and met loads of people that I'm still in contact with. We'd talk about buying land, running a business, opening a hostel, maybe doing a jerk beef business, washing cars, all sorts of stuff. There was a real entrepreneurial spirit there. You'll see people starting up businesses in Colombia and they're some of the most intrepid entrepreneurs that you'll meet. They wouldn't call themselves that, but they definitely are entrepreneurs in the way that they work. Anyway, I eventually met this really charming English guy out there, and he pulled me into this mountain biking business he was involved with. I jumped straight into it, as I'd always loved mountain biking, and I just knew it was going to be a massive success. So, we bought a jeep, we bought bikes, and we started running this company. We were running bikes down this mountain, through four ecosystems, down two and a half thousand metres through the jungle and out to the ocean. We'd also do jungle tours, canyoning tours, coffee tours, bird watching, indigenous experiences with local farmers, all these amazing things. It was a mind-blowing time. A lot of people who came on these tours would tell me that it was one of the best things they'd done in life, too. It was amazing to hear that, it really was.

Though the business sounded like a great idea, and I really believed in it, that first year was hard. It was probably one of the hardest years of my life. I was always working, barely getting any sleep, and I'd just started a new relationship. To add to that, I caught dengue fever out there and that almost killed me. I got through it and the second year, that was great. We built a great team and started getting a lot of recognition for our efforts. We were on government sponsored tourism promotions, in airline magazines, and we'd built up some cool connections. We did have some issues with partners initially, as they were just taking money out of the business and not letting it grow, but we worked through that and got new investors involved. It was a big celebration at the time, and we felt like we were flying.

While those new investors seemed happy with what we were doing, I started having problems with them when I wasn't around. I had to return to the UK at one point, and I left one of them to run the business. So, this older, lovely guy that had always been amazing with us, took over from me. Unfortunately, as soon as I left and there was money involved, he went a little crazy. He accused the staff of stealing things, tried to sack everyone, wanted to re-design the tours, then changed the configuration on the bikes. All sorts. This was something we'd built up over three years and he comes in and tries to change everything in the first week. We had these angry emails back and forth where I was asking him to stand back until I arrived back in the country. He couldn't accept that, couldn't trust anyone. This dude wouldn't leave things alone, so I snapped and told them to take their money back and that I was done with the business. After everything I'd done to save it, I just couldn't face more years of battle. We liquidated the business after that, and I stayed in Scotland.

NICOLA – CANADA

We moved to Canada last summer, to Kitchener to be precise, myself and my boyfriend at the time. It was more his dream, to be honest. His grandparents split up before he was born, one stayed in the UK and the other came to Canada, so he had family out here. After visiting them a few times, he decided he'd like to spend a couple of years living out here and seeing what it was all about. To be fair to him, he did mention this when we first got together, but I initially had no real interest in it. As the time went on though, I just thought, 'Why not?' I had nothing holding me back, no real ties other than family, so agreed to give it a go. We applied for working holiday visas, giving us two years of unlimited travel opportunities and the right to legally work, secured them, and moved out in the July.

I'll be honest, my intentions were always to return to the UK. I was happy to give it a go for his sake, but I always saw myself going back home at the end of the two years, if not sooner. What didn't help, was that I started working as a nanny out there, and I really didn't enjoy it. I was working for a family with five kids, and they were awful at times. I felt lonely, too. I'm a very sociable person and talking to people, seeing friends and family, that all makes me happy. Yet working as a part-time nanny, my only interactions would be with kids under nine years-old, so they don't hold much of a conversation. I wasn't getting paid very much, either, so we weren't really exploring our area or seeing the best of the country. I'd work, come home, and then do it all again the next day. I just thought, 'Why am I here?' It felt like I'd just swapped one job for another, just in a new country. So, there were times at the start when I wasn't in the greatest mental state, and definitely considered just going back home and being done with it all.

People kept telling me that the gap between your third

and sixth months away are the hardest, but it's not until I was through the other side that I could relate to that. Those first three months, you feel like you're on holiday and everything is fresh and exciting. Then you settle into life, your routines start again, and you being noticing the things you're unhappy about. That happened to me, for sure.

What changed though, was that I broke up with my boyfriend. I did it on Christmas Eve, five months after arriving, which wasn't the best timing on my part. If I'm honest, I think I was having doubts about the relationship before moving here. I'm quite a go getter, I want to go out, to explore, to do new things. Whereas he was always quite happy to just get here, to settle into a job, find an apartment, and take his time. So, you had someone concerned about saving money, whereas I was there for the new experiences. We had that constant battle throughout. I guess I thought moving to Canada might change that between us, but unfortunately it didn't. It got worse, if anything. I think, when I broke up with him, it was because I had that intention of moving back to England. I thought I shouldn't drag that out any longer, and it didn't really feel fair on either of us. I could've picked a better time, but the reason wouldn't have changed for me.

The thing is, after breaking up, I found myself enjoying life in Canada far more. I started to meet new people, became more independent, did things I wouldn't normally do. I also went on a few dates, found people who understood my sarcasm more, and just started being myself again. I found I was no longer adapting my personality to fit in, to stop trying to come down to someone's level so I could be accepted by them. That mindset shift, it made me see that I didn't want to waste this great opportunity. I also stepped back and saw that maybe the reason I wanted to go home wasn't because I was unhappy in the country, but because I was unhappy with him. He was great about it, though, and we do still live near each other now, so there are no ill feelings or bad words to say about him. We just wanted different things from our relationship.

I'm still in Kitchener today. I work part time in the morning doing accounts for a welding workshop, and when the world is running normally, I lead painting classes in the evening. This company is more like a night out, if anything. It's not teaching fine art skills, exactly. We host it in a restaurant or a bar, and it's usually up to thirty people. They all get their own canvas and paint, and then I teach them one specific painting that night. It's just a nice night out, something different. You can eat something, have a drink, learn some painting. It's a really sociable job and I love doing it.

I can honestly say that moving to Canada has changed me as a person. It's completely changed me, really. It made me leave my comfort zone, but at the same time become so much more comfortable with being myself and showing my personality. It's funny, I moved out here because it was someone else's dream. Yet I'm now the one that wants to stay, whereas he's considering going back home. I hope I can stay here, too.

JASON – AUSTRALIA

From working at a doctor's surgery in the New Forest for a long time, I'd become quite an insular type of person and stuck in a bit of a hole. I'd say I was quite depressed, very anxious, and it took me a long time to realize that I needed to change things about my life. I ended up taking a few holidays to America, just to get away for a bit, and they really helped. The first was to San Francisco, where seeing new places and even losing a bit of weight really helped me gain a load of confidence. I also met an Australian girl there, who I kept in touch with, but at the time nothing much came of that. Then, I took a second trip out to America and went hiking on the East Coast. Again, meeting other people and seeing what life could be like outside of my own bubble was really enlightening. I also met someone there, an American, and we were looking for places where we could stay together and still work. For British and American citizens, New Zealand looked like a good option, and I really bought into the idea. Those trips, they just made me realise how beautiful the world is and that there was more to life than sitting in that doctor's surgery back home. In the long term, we actually broke up, me and the American, but I wanted to go ahead with the New Zealand idea on my own anyway.

My relationship with the UK is interesting. When I did finally leave it, even just for those holidays, I already felt like I was looking for something else. I think you just get used to where you're from, but you might not know if you like or dislike it until you can compare it with somewhere else. When I got back from America, I just really wanted to leave the UK and find that somewhere else. I don't think I ever felt settled at home again, really. I'd learned to adapt to new places, to change my lifestyle, to have a bit of a plan. So, I sorted myself out with a working holiday visa for New Zealand for a year, where I was going to work for as long as I could, and another for Canada as a second option. Canada wasn't a guarantee at the time, as I thought I could also just go back to the UK if I wanted to. So, I planned this trip to New Zealand, including a stop off in Perth in Australia to meet the girl I met in San Francisco, and another stop in Brisbane to stay with some family. I thought it was a shame to fly all that way and not see these people, really. I'd never been to this part of the world, so I put everything into one trip in case I never came back.

Anyway, when I got to Perth, I spent a week getting shown around by my friend. And to be honest, I really liked her, so much so, that at the end of the week, I pitched the idea of coming back and seeing if being a couple would work. I did continue onto Brisbane and New Zealand as I planned, but it gave her some time to think it over, and then a bit more time for me to look into the visas. So, at one stage, I had valid visas for three countries, Australia, New Zealand, and Canada, and the option of just going back home. Going from that doctor's surgery, to suddenly having these options, that was quite a mindset shift for me. I definitely hadn't planned it out this way, nor had I planned to never go back home. Of course, moving to the other side of the world for a relationship, that did come with some pressure. I was thinking about it and wondering what I'd do if we broke up. I wouldn't have a place to stay locally, not while I was still looking for more stable work, but obviously that's not my intention here.

Living in Perth, it's great, but it's a difficult city to compare to anywhere else. It's apparently the most isolated city in the world, as it's out on the West coast of Australia and nowhere near another city. As a result, it spans for miles and doesn't feel over-crowded in the slightest. I hadn't expected to like it, as I'm not really a city person, but I can genuinely say it's one of the only cities I've ever enjoyed. The others are often too cramped, too dirty, and there's too many people in them. Perth is nothing like that, though. You do have the inner-city area, but even that has these nice parks and a big river running through it. There isn't that same sense of being on busy tube trains or surrounded by high-rise apartment blocks and the like. This place just has more of a positive, accepting vibe to it. Maybe not politically, but that's a different story. There's a lot of beaches, there's a lot of focus on outdoor areas due to the nice weather. I've met more of my neighbours along this street in the last year, than in the entire time I lived on my street in England. I think that says quite a lot about Australian hospitality as well.

I think a lot of people believe that they live in the best place in the world, but I honestly feel like I do live there currently. I'm close enough to the city centre, I'm close enough to the beach, I can get to an airport within thirty minutes. I can do everything I want around here. Is it paradise, though? I don't know, but it seems close enough to me.

CHRISTOPHER - GERMANY

I left school at seventeen and briefly studied to be a chemist. Well, for about three months anyway. The thing is, I was studying and working at the same time and it was all too much for me. I couldn't hack it, so just stopped. My mother knew the owner of this company though and got me a job as a trainee computer operator instead. Those were the days when we had huge computers in rooms with air conditioning to cool them down. They'd only have a fraction of the power of an iPhone today, though. I soon became a shift leader there and it was okay, nothing spectacular. When I was twenty though, I had my first little crisis in life and was just sat there thinking how bored I was. It seemed my life was going to be all about being successful in that job, then naturally I'd need to meet a girl, get married, buy a house, and have children etc. For me, I decided there must be far more than just that. So, while sat in this mundane computer centre, I started learning German, just for something to do, give me a different focus. It kept me entertained, but I was still dreadfully bored with this way of life and decided I didn't want to sit that out for the next forty years.

At the time, I was living at home with my parents and I felt like I just needed to emancipate myself from them and get away. I gave my notice at work, bought an interrail ticket, and set off. The thing was, for some odd reason I'd decided to pack my huge rucksack full of the books I was planning to read on the trip. I could barely walk; it was that heavy. Fortunately, when I was on my way to the tube, I met a mate there, and ended up giving him most of the books so he could drop them off with my Mum. After that dodgy start, I ended up in Norway, Sweden, hitched across Lapland, including being dropped off in the middle of the tundra, and then eventually settled at a job in a youth hostel in Garmisch-Partenkirchen in Germany. I decided I wanted to climb the mountains there, so taking a job nearby seemed like the best idea at the time.

Unfortunately, I ended up working a lot and barely climbing at all. I was too tired on my days off to go up the mountains, so I only lasted three months there. I did have this goal of then hitching all the way to Australia, but that wasn't really happening, and I was quickly running out of money. So, before I knew it, I was at the job centre in Munich, asking if they had any computer operator work going. I got a job at the first place I went to, found a room to rent, and there I was, living in Munich. I think I was a little bit lonely at the beginning, though it felt like loneliness crossed with adventure at the same time. To try to fix that, I went into the English pub a few times, but it just felt like it was full of people pretending to still be in England, so I soon stopped going. I stuck it out, found my place in the city, and it was working well for me.

By the time I was thirty-eight, I had another little crisis about my life and ended up moving to Bonn. I was in a strange relationship at the time, and when I was made redundant, I just took the package and got out of the relationship. The first role I found after that was in Bonn and for a while I'd commute on a weekly basis between the cities, but I eventually stayed here. It was a fun time, though. I was single again, which was rare, so I started doing things I'd always wanted to do. I started acting, then I joined a choir, I took dance lessons, went to writing classes, learned to ride a motorbike, that sort of thing. If anything, it was a typical midlife crisis, really. It was good for me, though. I was just enjoying myself. I also started playing for the Bonn Players, an English-speaking theatre group in the city, and I really enjoyed it.

I'm grateful for that period of my life, as it introduced me to what I call my retirement profession. The thing is, you go through life thinking you're still a teenager, that you're still eighteen, and then suddenly you're retiring. I've never liked the idea that you work for a long time, have a bit of a rest, and then die. That framework, it just doesn't work for me. By the time I was fifty-five, I just thought to myself, 'Is that it? Is that everything I get?' Fortunately, I worked out that it wasn't, that it was time for me to have the third stage of my life. So, I stopped working just before I was sixty, enrolled in a drama school, and I'm just about to graduate. It might sound strange, but I really felt like I needed a new profession between the ages of sixty and ninety. I felt like I needed to do something with my life, not just sitting around, and acting is that thing for me now.

I'm very happy in Bonn, it's a wonderful and diverse town and I'm really pleased that I live here. It's opened me up to these great opportunities and I'm trying to take them with both hands.

TODD – SOUTH KOREA & CAMBODIA

I worked for an IT company in Reading and they paid for my degree, basically. I did my undergraduate course while working, and the third year was incredibly intense. Trying to write my dissertation, to do my job, and have a social life at the same time, that just wasn't possible. I really had to sacrifice my social life and put that on hold for the year to make it all happen. Coming out the other side of that, I was a little burned out and wanted a break, so I asked my work for a sabbatical and they accepted it. I then took the chance to go traveling for the best part of nine months. For the last three months of that, I volunteered as an English teacher in Cambodia and absolutely loved it. I just built up a really good rapport with the students there and the whole experience made me feel good about myself. Before traveling, I didn't really have that much confidence, you see. I wasn't comfortable with social situations, with talking to girls, that sort of thing. And being out there, meeting new people, that really took me out of my comfort zone and taught me so much about myself.

Goodbye Britain

The problem is, when I got back to England I just despised being stuck behind a desk and working with computers again. I knew I had to see out my contract, as they'd paid for my degree, but I ended up handing in my resignation as soon as I realistically could. What added to that, was the Brexit vote. I was pretty devastated with that, to be fair. I was in France at the time it happened, watching football with some friends, and I remember telling them that I'd definitely be leaving the UK as soon as I could. Lots of people were saying that at the time, but I knew I'd see it through. I'd been thinking about teaching abroad again, and having been friends with someone with Korean heritage, I was always pretty fascinated by the things they told me about South Korea. Some good, some bad, some really interesting. So, I thought I'd try teaching over there and found myself a job at a private school in Busan and gave it a go.

At first, I thought the place was fantastic. There were lights everywhere, the bars were all open late, everything was so convenient. The country just works. Everything is quick, you'll get food instantly in a restaurant and it's cheap, too. So, my first impressions were good. The language barrier was a bit of a culture shock, though. I can speak a little now. I used to work at public schools and none of the Korean teachers could speak any English, so it forced me to speak Korean to them. The problem is, you've got things like subject and object markers and we don't use these in English, so there's a whole new concept that you need to get your head around, too. That and the hangul alphabet, obviously.

South Korea is a country that's come a very long way, in a very short space of time. It used to be an aid receiver, back in the 1960s, and by 2010 it had turned itself around and became an aid donor. I think that's pretty impressive. The thing is, on a social level, some of the country has been left behind. It's playing catch up, a little. A good example of that, is that you can still legally discriminate here. So, it's legal to discriminate on the grounds of gender, age, disability, religion, and sexuality. There's no laws against that, whatsoever. In general, the majority of the population aren't against that changing, but the issue of being more inclusive for LGBTX people, that seems to be the biggest sticking point for a lot. You see, the church still holds a lot of power here, and they're obviously against the idea that these people should be considered as equal. Then the political parties aren't keen to stand against the church, so nothing really changes. I think that upsets the younger generation, as they're keen to move forward and have a modern, inclusive society in South Korea.

I have a Korean girlfriend here, but because of the way the older generation view foreigners, I'm yet to meet her parents. They're okay with people coming here if they're willing to learn the language, to adapt to the culture, and to integrate. I think that's fair enough and I'm already doing that myself. But marrying their children? That's something they're really not happy with. So, I've been with my girlfriend for two and a half years now, but there's very little chance of me meeting her parents as it stands. I think she's reluctant to introduce them to a foreigner unless we want to get married, and even then, I think it'll end in a big argument. There are more intercultural marriage happening, though. That's a good thing, I think, as the birth-rate is currently one of the lowest in the world. So, they're either going to have to rely on immigration or to change policies to encourage having children. The thing is, there's this tradition for women to get married, have children, and settle down before they're thirty here. That's completely out of line with younger Korean culture now, though. The younger women aren't in a rush to get married or raise children, as the government don't do enough to support young women. They haven't provided adequate laws to help women return to work, for example. It can be a little bit backwards in that respect.

Despite these issues, I am really happy here. I've got a

good life, I've got good friends, I like my job, I've progressed my career, and I even play football. I think South Korea is a country moving in the right direction, too. I think over time, my generation will start to become those making the decisions here, and I do think that will lead to this country being increasingly progressive. Whereas when I look back at the UK right now, I feel like it's becoming a lost cause. I hope it doesn't continue like that, but I don't see much evidence of that changing.

CHANGING SCENERIES

BARBARA - SPAIN

I went to Spain to get over a broken heart. I'd been with my boyfriend for three years before then, an African guy who was very much my first love, but unfortunately, he went back to Kenya and got married to a local girl. It left me absolutely heartbroken. I was seriously depressed then and, in those days, they didn't have things like anti-depressants, so you just had to get on with it. It took me a long time to crawl out of the black hole that I was in. I just wanted to do something that stopped me from sitting around thinking about my problems.

Initially, I tried to throw myself into my job. I'd just completed my teacher training course and found myself teaching at a comprehensive school in Fife. They'd just raised the leaving age from fifteen to sixteen then, and I was given the kids that should've left school already. Most of them didn't want to be there and it was difficult. They give you the worst kids when you start, which is a bit silly. You still had to use corporal punishment in those days, and I had to buy a leather strap myself. I was expected to use it, too. It all just left me very unhappy. I felt like I was stuck in this awful rut and I really wasn't sure if I wanted to stay in teaching after that. I thought I'd take a year out, go abroad for a break, and then think about going into social work or probation on my return.

I wanted to go somewhere that I didn't know the language, so was looking at Italy and Spain. I didn't think I could cope with the Italians, so took some advice from some Spaniards I knew and ended up in Barcelona as an English teacher. I didn't know any Spanish before I went, and my Mum said she didn't think I knew what I was signing up for until I was already going. I looked as white as a sheet as I left the train station that day, apparently. I was like that though; I'd take a decision and then suddenly wonder what I'd done. So, off I went with my ten words of Spanish and a week of 'Learning to teach English' behind me, and I was living in Barcelona on my own.

This was in 1975 and before mobile phones or the internet, so I felt quite isolated at first. I felt a long way from home at times, but I knew I couldn't give up and go back there. It would've been expressing failure, to admit that I hadn't achieved anything. I couldn't do that. I just found the idea of learning a language, making friends, that sort of thing, to be hard. There's something in me that forces me to do it, though. I knew I needed to break that miserable cycle and busy myself with teaching, planning my lessons, occupying my broken heart for as long as I could. Eventually, that started to work for me.

After three years in Barcelona, which was longer than I'd initially planned to stay, I'd made some friends, found a nice boyfriend, and learned a bit of Spanish. I'd also started to enjoy the job, but the pay wasn't great, and I needed to find a way to kick on. It seemed the best way was to return to the UK, get a teaching diploma, and then head back out. So, I did that, but this time I ended up in Madrid.

I didn't really have any friends in that city when I arrived, so I was trying to find accommodation on my own. I went to this woman's house and she showed me around the room. The problem was, there was a huge crucifix hanging over the bed. She told me I couldn't have men over, even just friends, as the neighbours would gossip. She said she'd go to a hotel for 'that sort of thing', despite it being her own home. I didn't think that was the right place for me. Back then, you'd often be pointed out as being the loose foreigner, though. I'd be called *La Rubia*, the blonde one, or *La Extranjera*, the foreign one. It didn't help that the Spanish girls had to be home by 10pm, either. If you were going out with a Spanish guy, you were pretty sure he had a Spanish girlfriend too if he'd only see you after 10pm. It was all part of the experience, though.

I've always been a big live music fan and it was an exciting time to be in Madrid. You could see these amazing bands for barely any money. We had a socialist mayor at the time, and he'd put on all these concerts during the Madrid fiestas in May. I saw Tina Turner for a fiver, Van Morrison, David Bowie, Elton John. I'd also go to this little club up the road and the see the likes of Echo and the Bunnymen and Simple Minds. They were number one in the UK back then, but they hadn't caught on in Spain. As the music changed, so did the country in general. I was no longer being treated as a stranger, and Madrid became a very tolerant city to live in.

I stayed in the city for twelve years. One Easter, I came back to the UK to do a course. I'd never been home at that time of the year before, but I was staying at these halls of residence that overlooked a field of daffodils. I hadn't seen daffodils for over a decade, and I just suddenly felt this overwhelming longing to be back in the UK. As impetuous as I am, I just went back to Spain after the course and said, 'That's it, I'm going back.' Within a month, I had a job in Colchester. I had no idea where that was though, so I had to ask people. But I was interviewed for this role there, got it, and found myself living in Essex before I knew it.

I enjoyed my time in Spain, though not all of it. In retrospect,

I wish I'd stayed less time there. I wish I'd spent less time on certain relationships too, but that's it. You can't change your life now, it's happened, and you just need to get on with it.

HELEN - AUSTRALIA & NEW ZEALAND

I just hate absolutely everything about the UK. Particularly the weather, I really hate the weather. I don't like the rain and I really hated the winters there, too. Whereas on the other hand, I love the sun out here in Australia. If anything, I must be part reptile as it gets to forty degrees here and I'm sat quite snug. But while the weather was fundamentally one of the reasons why I left, it wasn't the only issue. I also dislike the culture and many of the people. I dislike making stupid people famous. I know it happens everywhere, but the UK is crazy for it. Watching Love Island is my idea of absolute hell, but it seemed to be the national pastime. Nothing about that place appeals to me, and I'm not sorry about saying that out loud, either.

Before I left for the first time, I was living in a flat in London that had the A4 on one side, the tube on the other. It had cockroaches and my neighbours were a bloody nightmare. I had no outdoor space, either. I just couldn't see my way out of it in the UK. Flats weren't cheap and even though I had one, because of where it was, I couldn't move anywhere else. It was a very privileged problem to have, but I was just absolutely miserable. I then got made redundant from the magazine I was working on, and suddenly the idea of moving abroad seemed more feasible. I didn't have a job to leave, so there wasn't this 'Oh my god, what am I doing?' feeling at the back of my mind, so I thought I'd take my chances and head to the other side of the world. I moved just after the terrorist attacks on September 11th, that was the date of my moving party. It was too late by then to worry about getting on a plane, though.

Changing Sceneries

I went to live in New Zealand with my ex-boyfriend at first. He'd grown up there, yet somehow had fewer qualifications to live there than me, so I took him back with me. I have no idea where we stayed at first, but we soon got a short-term apartment while house hunting. At the time, I was able to sell my crap hole in London with all the cockroaches, and effectively trade it for a three-bedroom house with two hundred- and seventy-degree views of Auckland harbour. It was a dream house and one that I never thought I'd be able to buy. Beautiful views, no neighbours, huge rooms with six-foot paintings on the walls. I still can't believe it. And that was just the profit from my shitty flat I sold in London.

On the job front, I went with the intentions of working for some papers there, but then I saw the pay and thought better of it. Fortunately, I had enough clients back in the UK from being freelance, so just continued doing that. And the good thing about New Zealand, is that it really calmed me down. The internet was there, and we all had an email address, but it wasn't as hectic as it is now. Newspapers weren't online, nor were magazines, and if people wanted my work, they had to wait for me. I think I was close to a major breakdown back home, as I'd just take whatever work was going and often it was all at the last minute. It works both ways, though. My Mum used to go to the newsagent every week and package up magazines and newspapers and send them up to me. Then literally a week later, a parcel would arrive with that previous week's news for me to catch up with. It was fun, that's for sure.

I got bored after six years, though. It's fantastic, a gorgeous place to live, and it probably saved my sanity. However, after a while I wanted all the things that I'd tried to move away from. I wanted more than one pub, I wanted friends who had glamorous jobs, I wanted to be more into media, I wanted that city feel again. I went to a hen party there and it was in the afternoon and no-one was drinking, possibly because the bride was pregnant but that's beside the point. We had this competition to see what the weirdest thing was in your handbag. I had a temporary tattoo, weirdly, and someone else had a tapestry kit. And she won. So, I just thought, 'Okay, I'm off.' That was the defining moment for me, and I just decided I was moving to Sydney. It was either Sydney or Melbourne, but Melbourne can get cold and has seasons, so I went to Sydney.

Nowadays, life has caught up in New Zealand. It's not possible to do what I did. House prices have caught up, they're now three times as much. I'm sure they've caught up with reality tv, too. At the time though, it was a completely different world. The people weren't materialistic, possessions didn't matter to them as much, they weren't judged by their handbags or looks, or even what they do for a living. People just judged you on who you were as a person. I didn't even wear shoes for six years, just flipflops the whole time. You could walk into the nicest restaurant in jeans and no one would care, they'd just be interested in whether you're a nice person or not.

GARY – LATVIA

When you tell people you're moving to Latvia, their first question is often, 'Where?' I'd also get, 'You're going to Russia?' too. So, it's an instant geography lesson for people. They're then quite inquisitive and keen to ask questions. I suppose it's not a country that rolls off everyone's tongue all the time, is it? Obviously to friends and family, it wasn't a great surprise. They knew I was in a relationship with a Latvian, but I guess the natural expectation was that the Latvian would want to move to the UK. She wasn't in search of work though, but one of us had to move to a new country if we were to be together.

In truth, I loved the UK, so it really wasn't that I was looking to move away. I worked in IT at the time and travelled the country frequently, seeing all its highs and lows, and all its beauty. Sure, I was stuck in a car the whole time and living half of my life in hotels and guest houses, but I still loved it. So much so, that I'd only been on a foreign holiday once before, then lost my passport after that and never bothered to replace it. Yet within a year of meeting my future wife, I decided I'd come out to Riga and try living a life out here. So, I left my job on the Friday, met my now wife for the first time on the Monday, and started freelancing from Latvia that week.

I'm not really a city person and I never wanted to live in London, but Riga felt like a nice in-between. It's a city with great infrastructure and good public transport, but you could still escape to the countryside. For the three years we were there together, I really liked it. I started building a business back in the UK though, so eventually we did find ourselves back there and living in Norfolk for ten years. My wife would come back over to Latvia on regular visits to see her parents during this time. They live on a homestead, or what some call a small holding, and it's in the middle of nowhere. Unfortunately, on what was her last visit, her father fell over and broke his hip. It left her stuck there, caring for him. He was in his eighties by then and we really didn't know whether he'd survive or not. He's still going, and going, and going right now, but it did get to the stage where we had to make a permanent decision. So, we packed up and moved over here for a really different life.

Homesteading has been a huge adjustment, but I'm quite a planner and I like to do my research. In terms of life, this wasn't as "drop everything and come" as it sounds. We'd planned the idea out for a while, and I'd started watching YouTube videos about various topics to make sure I was ready. I was watching all these videos on growing your own food, living remotely, tree management, that sort of thing. I felt like I'd been to agricultural college by the end of it all, but it also helped my transition. We have a fifty-hectare plot here, of which the vast majority is managed forest. When the time is right, it's cut down and replanted, and we've been through one of those already. We had to plant over one thousand trees ourselves!

Prior to moving here, I think about thirty percent of what was eaten was grown on the property. Meat was always an issue, but a fish and meat dealer would show up once a week and you'd buy from them. Then, we had this crazy idea to get a couple of pigs and do some pig husbandry. They're fairly easy to look after, but they have quite a character. We went out to the middle of nowhere and bought these two pigs, and on the way home one of them escaped out of the carrying case. I looked in the rear-view mirror, and there it was, looking back at me in the road. Everyone we spoke to said we were absolutely mad. We raised these two pigs and when it came to slaughter them, we did that too. So, we experienced everything for the first time. The night before one was due to be slaughtered, it escaped. I looked out of the front door and there was a pig grazing. So, it was never a dull moment.

We're coming to what's known as the hunger gap. If you're self-sufficient, you must be clever in working out what you can grow to be ready for this. We've got a big basement, so we can store a lot of this stuff, but we must really focus on what we're growing and making sure we're ready. It just takes planning, being prepared, and knowing how to navigate the seasons. The growing season is short here, so you've only got three or four months to do it all. You have to be multi-skilled and you have to learn to make-do. Sometimes it's a bit like that scene in Apollo 13 where they throw all this stuff on a table and they needed to make something out of it. In real life, living here, it's either a situation where nothing is open, or it's the middle of winter. I'll give you one example; there wasn't running water here until two years ago and previously the water was brought in via buckets. But suddenly that pump failed, and we had to work out how to fix it, just using whatever we had. It was certainly a challenge, but something I've come to enjoy.

Latvia itself can be a very introverted country, but as soon as you go into someone's house then you're very looked after. The hospitality might be humble, but it's excellent. I've also found that people can be suspiciously curious as to why you're here, but you can break through that. It's a very patriotic and nationalistic country, too, but it does that in a really, really nice way. It understands its culture and history in a way that perhaps Britain doesn't. There's a big emphasis on its' food and its' dancing. In fact, there's a big national dance festival every four years and it's a huge undertaking. Latvia's song and dance heritage is really, really strong. My daughter, who now goes to Kindergarten here, has national dance and costume lessons that are paid for by the state. Every child has that option here, so they learn the dance and understand what to wear. I think learning that as small child is a fantastic experience.

I think people come here for a quieter life. That's fair enough, but most of them will still live in the city. Living out here, working on our own land, it's challenging but really rewarding. We're benefitting from the work that my wife's ancestors have put in. Hopefully my daughter's children will benefit from our work, too. Her inheritance isn't just bricks and mortar, but a living inheritance. It's certainly an interesting way to live.

ANN – SOUTH AFRICA

We're from working class backgrounds in the UK, from the Yorkshire Dales. We married very young, had our children very young, and we were struggling. There were strikes across the country during that Thatcher era, and in general it just wasn't a great time for the working class. I was working evening shifts in pretty awful jobs. One in a cotton mill and another in a fish and chip shop. My husband would work nightshifts on the shop floor for a car manufacturer, come home and sleep all day, and then in the evening we'd both leave for work again. It wasn't much of a life now I've come to think about it. We'd barely see each other, too.

My sister-in-law, she already lived in South Africa and was always encouraging us to come over. Then one day, I saw an advert in a national paper for the same job my husband was doing but this was based in South Africa. He applied for that and we toddled off to York for the interview. I was extremely nervous about the whole thing, I just felt so young and inexperienced. They really put us at ease though and told him he had the job, just like that. So, we sold everything we'd owned, all our furniture, and then went with four large suitcases full of clothes. I was scared to death, though. I was terrified. It was the first time we'd even flown, let alone to Africa of all places.

When we landed, you had to walk down the steps onto the tarmac. All I recall seeing as we emerged, was the army with guns. I'd never seen a gun in my life before then. I was absolutely terrified, and I had my two little boys with me. I just told my husband I was going back home, that I wasn't staying. I tried to get back up the stairs, but the air hostess stopped me, and my husband eventually got me into the airport in a bit of a state.

I just didn't like it there at all, I really wasn't happy at the start. If I'm honest, I actually hated it with a passion. It was too hot for me, I was on my own with the kids during the day, and I was just mourning the loss of my family. I was always very close to them, and then I suddenly didn't have their support and didn't get to see them all the time. It was needs must for us though, we just couldn't afford to go back.

Moving during the apartheid, we really weren't aware of it at the time. We had no idea how awful it was. The government in South Africa, they made sure it was covered up. Once we started experiencing it first-hand, it was just shocking beyond belief. We had all these African ladies coming up to our gates asking for work, and it wasn't until our friends started employing them that we gave it a go. We had a lovely lady working for us for many, many years, and I'd chat to her about it. If a white South African had walked in then, they'd have been beside themselves, I'm sure. I once told someone at work that our helper had used my bathroom and they were absolutely horrified. People wouldn't come to my house after that, all because I'd let a black person use my bath. The thing is, most of these women lived on the properties they worked in, and they'd often have their own showers to use but normally just with cold water. That felt cruel to me, so I let her use our bathroom. The treatment of these people, it was as bad as you can imagine. It was shocking beyond belief, really. Anyone who said it wasn't, they're lying.

To be fair to my husband's company, they said during the interview that we needed three years to really find our feet and settle in the country, and they were right. We realized that we just needed to make the most of it and eventually we started to have a much better life than we'd had in the UK. We managed to buy a car, buy a house, get good jobs, send our boys to school. I also became very ambitious here and worked my way up the ranks in the company I joined, working there for thirty years.

You never quite fit in here, I'll be honest. You're never going to be fully accepted with a British accent. I don't have a broad Yorkshire accent, but I don't have a South African one either and it means I'm never going to be fully accepted. You end up making your own world around your children and their children, just to have your own sense of identity. I think the worst thing I've found, or the thing that hit me pretty hard, was when I went back to the UK and I didn't fit in there either. I'm caught in between, really. I'm different now. I've lived through things and I've seen things that they haven't. A lot of British people have lived in their small towns their whole life and they just don't get out of it. They might go on holiday to Spain, or in years gone by to places like Blackpool or Scarborough, but that's for a week and then they return. I've found that really hard to comprehend.

Despite that, we strongly considered moving back to the UK, but then our grandchildren arrived, and we decided we couldn't leave them. Now, our South African Rand is effectively worthless, and we'd lose too much if we tried to go back. We'd have to live in a pokey little flat and I'd have to have my dogs with me, so that just wouldn't work, would it? So, this is where we'll be. We're happy here now and our grandchildren make it complete.

RICHARD – USA

I've always been the person who was never happy with where they were. Growing up in a small village near Newmarket, I was the first in my family to go off to university. Then I was the first person in my group to leave Suffolk and move to London. I was bored back home, really, there was just nothing for me there. I always had these ideas to go somewhere bigger, more exciting, more relevant to me. So, I moved to London, and eventually started working for a motion graphic animation company for bands on tour. If you go to a big concert at an arena and there's some crazy animations on screen behind them, there's a chance that I made it. It's a role that I still enjoy today, too. It's also given me a lot of opportunities, which I'm sure we'll get onto.

After being in London for ten years though, it starts to wear you down, you know. And I just got to the point where I was fed up with the train every day, I hated being on that packed carriage with everyone looking down and being miserable. Then when you're above ground, it's always grey and horrible, too. I was also just sick of this permanently downbeat, negative attitude a lot of the people around me had. People moaning about their chips being down, but doing nothing about it? That just rubs me up the wrong way. There's so much cool shit going on everywhere, so why do we take such pleasure in complaining the whole time?

I just thought, I didn't need that in my life anymore. So, when my boss pitched the idea of expanding the company to America, I really didn't need much convincing.

I always liked that romanticised LA, Hollywood, sunny beaches vibe that you see in the movies. It does look really appealing as an English kid, doesn't it? It took me until I was 26 to actually go there though, and by that time I'd built it up to be this big, dream destination. Then I got out to Los Angeles on my first work trip, and I absolutely fucking hated it. The traffic was a nightmare, it took ages to get anywhere, there wasn't really any sights. All these things, it really wasn't how I imagined it to be. But then every time I'd come back for work, I loved it a little more. Living here for a week or two weeks at a time, I didn't feel that pressure to enjoy myself as a tourist. I'd be happy with going out for breakfast and lunch, just having drinks. There wasn't that constant need to get places, to see things, to make the most of it. And before long, I absolutely loved this city and was really excited to get the opportunity to switch from London and while getting paid to do it, too.

Unfortunately, that's partly what led to my divorce. I was married at the time and my ex-wife didn't want to move and leave her friends and family. She hated the idea of America. On the other side, this was my goal and my dream. It was the biggest move I could make it my career and my life. Eventually, it just ended in divorce as there was no way we could both get what we wanted. It was hanging over our marriage for a whole year before I moved, and I'll put my hands up and say that I didn't really consider her part in all of it. I was laser focused on myself and how I could achieve my big dream. So, when it was being handed to me, in a package, with a nice little bow on it, I just fucking took it. The way I handled it all, that lost me a lot of close friends. People picked sides and obviously I was the one coming across as an arsehole, so about eighty percent of those around me dropped away. Moving to another country was hard enough, but dealing with a divorce and losing friends, that definitely made it harder than I anticipated, I'll be honest. Would I do things differently if I had the chance? Probably, but I'd ultimately still have ended up living here.

When you're moving and living here, there's so much that you don't even consider. My friend who'd moved here previously, he told me that the first six months were the hardest and probably the worst I'd encounter. He told me I'd hate it, that it's gonna suck, that I'm going to want to leave. After that first six months, apparently everything would start to get easier. It's because you're coming from a culture that you grew up with, and suddenly you're planted in this other country where it seems similar on the surface, but it's actually far more complex than that. You know, speaking English, people just assume that you'll read a website and it'll all just work out. Ultimately, he was perfectly right. The first six months was the hardest thing I've ever done. I was not in a good place mentally, I had no one to talk to, I knew my friend and my boss out of three-hundred and seventy-five million people here. You suddenly feel like a very, very small fish in a very, very big pond. I just chipped away at it, and before long I was absolutely loving it here. I never thought I wanted to go back. I was very glad to be out. There was never a time where I thought I couldn't do it and just had to go home. I was having a hard time adjusting and getting myself set up, but I just never wanted to give in.

You know, moving here was the best decision I ever made. I don't see myself moving back to the UK at all, either. It's funny, I was walking down the road the other day, and someone had tagged 'Go home to Europe' on a wall. I just thought to myself, no way, have you not seen the state of that right now?

ELLA - TURKEY

I'm from Omagh and in 1998, after the bomb where we lost quite a few people, I just needed to get out of the country. I was in England for a while, but in the late 90's and around the time of the Good Friday Agreement, it wasn't great to have an Irish accent. I was in Manchester, which would normally be very tolerant of Irish people, but after the Manchester bombing, it was an awkward time. I think I just needed to get as far away from that as possible. It could've been easy for me to spiral out of control there, I reckon. Then one day, my friend just said, 'Do you wanna go to Turkey? Shall we go for six months and work on a language course?', so I agreed, and we went.

At the time, my Dad was totally against it. He helped me with the ticket money, but only after I gave him this big spiel about how I was a grown up and how I needed to be allowed to make my own mistakes. I was twenty at the time, so I thought I was really independent and ready for the world. I just didn't have the financial gubbins to back it up, though. He said he'd give me the money, but only enough for a single ticket. His idea was that if I was as grown up as I claimed, then I had to make it work for at least six months. He said he'd then pay for my return after that.

When we got there, it turned out to be a pretty small language course. There were only four foreigners, and what should've set us off was that they were all leaving. It turns out they weren't getting paid and there was us, two women, with no idea what we were doing. So, two weeks after I arrived, I ended up crying on the phone to my Dad, asking for the ticket money to get back home. He just reminded me that I was apparently an adult, so he was leaving me to it. I've always joked that anything that happened after that, it's really his fault. I got through it by picking up private lessons and stuff like that, but it was a rocky start.

The area of Turkey I live it, it's very active in the human trafficking trade, particularly with the number of prostitutes that come through here. I'd say around a quarter of the town was full of dirt-cheap hotels when I first arrived, and they'd call that the Russian quarter. And on my second day, I was told not to go there. I kept going on about it until someone, a human rights lawyer, told me what was happening. I thought it was because I'd get mugged, but it turns out that was where the girls were. The thing is, the city is in a great location for that, right next to the Georgian border. I've been through that border in the past and it's scary. There were people dressed in black with bullet proof vests, full armour, all sorts. This is coming from someone from Northern Ireland, as well. After that, I did work with women's groups here to help them get funding from the EU, to help women who are trying to escape. It's something that I'm very, very aware of now. If you've got sad, young girls looking out of windows, then it's a bit of a tell. When they get raided now, they're still lifting about 15-20 girls per raid, too.

With all that in mind, you're probably wondering why I'm still here, aren't you? At first, pride kept me here. It was pride, more than anything, really. In Northern Ireland, everyone emigrates. It's normally to Australia, America, New Zealand, that sort of thing. They go away, make their money, and then they come home and buy a house. That's what you do. With me, I'd have been ribbed if I went away for two weeks and then crawled back. I stayed because I got out of that job, found another teaching job, and then met the man who became my husband.

Whenever people think about Turkish men, they either think of the men with the beards or the greasy waiters you get in the Mediterranean part of the country. My husband is neither of them, though. He's a civil engineer for a start and a great guy. He did initially tell me he couldn't marry me, though. His family weren't happy that I wasn't a Muslim, whereas some of my family were worried because he was one. The Turkish side probably felt sorry for my husband. I'd imagine it was all, 'God love him, he's marrying a foreign woman, she can't cook, probably wears her shoes in the house, too.' On my side, people were pitying me, 'God love her, she's so far away, what's she going to do?' It took my family a while to come round to the idea, and even now after nineteen years my brothers are still readying a room for me to come back to live in.

TRISH - GERMANY

I was born in '44, so it was during the war. Now, apparently when I was four years old, I turned to my mother and said that I'd like to live in Germany when I was bigger. That surprised her, as you can imagine. It certainly wasn't a common sentiment in the late forties or early fifties, was it? By the time I was sixteen though, I was fluent in the language and spent a while in this country, initially for a school term but then I was offered a job out here and stayed for six months. I loved it, but I did have to leave eventually and go back home to the UK.

After school, I got a job at Gatwick airport, met a police sergeant there, got married, and had two kids by the time I was twenty-one. He was the wrong man, unfortunately. He wouldn't let me teach German to the kids, probably because he was worried that we'd talk about him behind his back, though. I also used to buy books in German, just to read the language, but I had to hide them from him throughout. It took me seventeen years to divorce him, but I'd always kept my love for the language and the country throughout those years.

I then married husband number two, but that was only for five years and then he died. Then I was onto husband number three. I know what you're thinking, I didn't leave many gaps in between, did I? Anyway, my daughter was living in Germany by then, having moved out there to be an au-pair, whereas we were living in Cornwall. It was thirty percent unemployment in the country then and a pretty difficult time for everyone. I did have a nice little job, but unfortunately my boss committed suicide and I ended up losing that job. My husband, he was only working in the bakery in a supermarket. So, between us, we didn't have much going on. Having previously been over to Dusseldorf for my daughter's wedding the year before, and both loved it, we figured we could give living there a go. We were living in a mobile home in Cornwall, sold up, packed a suitcase each, and moved into an attic at my daughter's friend's house near Dusseldorf. I got on that plane with ten grand smuggled around my body and in various parts of my underwear, which felt quite daring at the time.

My older sister, who was born just after the outbreak of the war, was horrified by the idea of me living in Germany. She said she'd never come and visit, and she didn't. The closest she got, was the Belgium border. I understood it, of course. My mother told me that some of her own friends had been killed in bombing raids, so that anti-German sentiment was pretty strong. You'd often hear people say things like, 'Why the fuck would you want to live with them?', too. That's the thing I've found with Britain, though. It's very much an island, which can make people very insular. It was the late '80s by the time we'd moved here, but people were still bringing up the bloody war all the time. It still happens today, too.

Both me and my husband, we were very lucky when it came to finding work here. My husband worked on the gate at the British army base and I worked for the translation department. We were there as civilians, but it worked well for us. I moved into different jobs after that first year. I had a job at a golf club, I worked for a marketing company, did some translation for a bit, before then settling back into a job in the army for the British Health Service. I worked there until I retired, or more like until they chucked me out. My husband worked there for his whole

German career as it were, before unfortunately passing away.
There were times when he wanted to move back to the UK, but
his work thought the world of him, and he was happy to stay for
my sake. I'll always love him for that, too.

Now one day, by pure coincidence, I discovered that the
British army had a theatre group and I joined up. I was at the
hospital and overheard someone talking about how they'd miss
an audition and my eyes just lit up. As a kid, and we're talking
about being two years old here, I'd already been on the stage.
I'd played a teddy bear in a show that my Mum had written. I
just had to say, 'My name is Tuppence', but I absolutely loved
it and absorbed as much of the theatre as I could then. I was
always hanging around backstage, getting in the way, being a
nuisance in the wings. Unfortunately, my first husband, the
one who wouldn't let me teach the kids German, he didn't like
me being on stage and put a stop to that. So, it wasn't until I
suddenly found this theatre group, that I was able to get back
into it. Apparently, I walked in and the two directors looked at
each other and said, 'Here comes our witch', and I got the part.
I stayed with them for about ten years and we went all over
Europe doing that and playing at drama festivals. I thoroughly
enjoyed it. I made costumes, I played leading roles, and it was
great.

Unfortunately, the British army then withdrew and went
home, so I was left without anything. Initially, I did think, 'Well,
shit, what am I going to do?' And that's when I googled how to
become an extra in Germany, as you do. It's gone absolutely
batshit, since. I've had speaking roles in three Hollywood
movies, I've played the voice of the Queen on a major German
TV show, I've landed parts in TV commercials. I'm not always
typecast as a grandma, either. I've been a mafia boss twice,
which was a lot of fun. I loved being a baddie, I'll admit.
Obviously, it's great to have bigger parts on TV and in movies,
but I don't mind being an extra. You get a day out. You'll get
paid probably one-hundred euros or more. You'll get your travel

expenses. You get to meet some great people. I really can't complain at all. For me, it's become the greatest hobby in the world. I'll occasionally get recognized on the street, too. I think that's fantastic. There are two or three elderly gentlemen who, now that I'm a widow, would apparently quite happily come over for a cup of coffee and a bit else. It's funny, but I take it all with a pinch of salt.

I have no idea if I'd have found these opportunities back in the UK, but I'm glad I found them in Germany.

JAMES – PORTUGAL

I'm on my second marriage and I met my Brazilian wife in London, having both been through some messy, difficult divorces. My ex-wife poisoned my kids against me, even if they're in their twenties, and as I was living in a fairly small town, I kept bumping into them and our friends all the time. So, I just wanted to get away. We came to Madeira on holiday, liked it, and just thought we should come over and live here. We came out for a month initially, rented a one-bedroom apartment right in the city centre, and started looking for our own place.

The city centre ended up being really noisy and the air quality was terrible there. They use all these old buses, and as they run on diesel, it just stinks of the stuff. So, we figured we'd look elsewhere. As it turns out, for the same price of a one-bedroom apartment in the city, we could probably get a three-bedroom house with a garden elsewhere on the island. We didn't have much joy at first though, and almost headed back to the UK for a few months, but we were then put in contact with an agent to see if she could help. It was funny at first, as I said I wanted a three-bed detached house, one where I could lie in bed and see the sea, and I didn't want to spend more than two-hundred grand on it. This girl, she just laughed and said I clearly didn't want much then, but within twenty-four hours she'd found us a place that ticked all the right boxes. Here, you sit with the solicitor, agree on the details, decide a handover date, and then pay ten percent of the asking price. We did all of that pretty quickly, at least in my mind. Me and my wife, we're quite impulsive people and before we knew it, we'd bought this place. It was a bit of a whirlwind. I was sat on the plane back home thinking, 'I can't believe I've just bought a house in Portugal.' The next thing you know, we've got all the papers, we're ordering a shipping container, and three weeks later we'd turned up and were moving in.

Madeira used to be a poor, little island, so people went across the world to try and make their fortune. A lot of them went to South Africa, then Brazil, then Venezuela. So now, there's a massive Brazilian community here and a decent number of Venezuelans, too. You'll also find that if people speak good English here, it's probably with a South African accent. Obviously, you've got some people speaking Portuguese with a bit of a Spanish accent and they tend to be the Venezuelan. What I like about it though, is that everyone mixes in. There's no racism or discrimination. The strange thing here is that when you drive on the motorway to the main city, there is no flat road. You're either on a viaduct or in a tunnel. Before the EU money came in to build the roads, the easiest way to get between places was by boat. So, you can get wildly different accents between the two towns, and culturally they can be quite different. Then, up in the mountains, you get completely different people. They're shorter, darker, wear different clothes. It's fascinating at times.

We didn't move to a tourist area here, we moved to where the locals live. The place was cheaper, the air is better, and some of the people around here are more humble and friendlier than in the tourist areas. If you go to the bank in town, for example, they're not much help. It's interesting, the poorer people seem more willing to speak English, and most of them have learned it from watching TV. My neighbours around here, they farm and chop wood down and sell that. They're all self-employed or self-unemployed, if you will. When we first moved here, you could see them all nudging each other and it was a bit of a novelty for them, but after going to the local bar a few times, getting to know them, really integrating, they've been great with us. They're all very, very friendly. Then where we are, there's no crime. You can go for a walk, leave your house unlocked, and there's no bother.

I was diagnosed with cancer here, unfortunately. I went to meet this English-speaking doctor, recommended by my wife, and he asked me when I last had my prostate checked. It had been a while, so he insisted checking, then took some blood samples, and sent them off. My son was then out here for my birthday, and while he was here, I got a call and was told to go back and see them immediately. Long story made short, they caught it just in time. Literally, just in time. My levels were so high, that if it spread anywhere, I'd have been in big trouble. So, I had MRI scans, CAT scans, bone scans, all sorts. I paid privately, but within two months I was lying in hospital after having everything removed. Touch wood, I'm 18 months beyond that. If I was in the UK, it might not have been picked up and I could be dead by now. I was very, very lucky. I'm very grateful for Madeira and the experiences I've had here, and very grateful for the doctor for doing his job so diligently.

ADAM - JAPAN

I was frustrated with the job, mate. I just took whatever role they'd give me after my internship, as most of us were doing back then. It ended up being bullshit, though. I was dealing with people I just didn't want to talk to and while living in London, which isn't ideal. I kinda hate London, if I'm honest. And living there on a really low wage, that's even worse. So, it just wasn't a good time. I sat there one day just thinking, 'I need to get out of this place' and came up with the idea to return to Japan. I'd been there previously, thought it was a good laugh, and was still young enough to get a working holiday visa to live there. I'd also just started working with a Japanese band who'd signed for a major label and were touring overseas, doing things like tour managing or interpreting for them, which was handy. So, I thought I'd go over, do some English teaching when I needed to, and then do these intermittent jobs with that band for the year.

While I was out here, I started doing some local tour management jobs for American bands who were in the country. I did one for a pretty big artist who was signed directly to my previous team in London, too, though she was relatively unknown in Asia at the time. Then, just as my working holiday visa was due to expire, literally on the day I was supposed to leave the country, the record label reached out to me again. I hadn't done any work for them for months, but they suddenly offered me a job. They'd just started an indie music label in Japan and didn't really know what to do with it. They were also under pressure to make it work and wanted someone who knew the business and could speak the language. I just took it, it kept me in the country, and I could earn pretty decent money from it at the same time. I was working on the localisation of overseas releases, so doing the marketing and the packaging. It was mainly indie-rock stuff. There was this idea that I'd pick up things from the rest of the label and try to make that work in Japan. You need to have a fully Japanese release, with all the lyrics in Japanese etc, for it to work, so I'd get involved in all of that. That was the idea, and I liked the sound of it enough to take it.

Having worked at a major label in the UK, there's always a good atmosphere and it often felt very much like you'd expect the music industry to feel. In Japan though, it was very corporate, very grey, and there's a lot of meetings where nothing seems to happen. Just people sitting around listening to someone talk for long periods, and it just didn't feel as vibrant or as exciting. I didn't enjoy it much in the UK as it was, and this felt very, very different and not very musical, to be honest. It was like working on a commodity. I felt like I was a supply chain manager, really. Maybe it's because I get bored of things quickly, but towards the end of the year I just realized it wasn't cool and it wasn't fun.

A month after I started the job though, the big earthquake happened here. I was initially quite blasé about it and was just sat in the café downstairs waiting it out like we'd often do. This time though, you had all these Japanese people screaming as it happened. From that, I knew it was something bigger. We went outside and you could see the buildings swaying, these huge buildings just rocking back and forth. It was surreal, like nothing I'd ever experienced before or since.

After the initial shock, I wasn't sure if I was just supposed to go back to my desk or not. Especially as you'd normally have aftershocks, but we all just went back inside. There were broken TVs, ceiling tiles on the floor, incredible amounts of paper everywhere. There were cracks in the stairwell walls, but as none of the buildings in the area were collapsing, we didn't seem in immediate danger. Once we turned the tv on though, we saw the tsunami was coming. I just remember thinking, 'Oh holy shit.' That's when the emergency broadcasts started, and there were announcements over the radio system. We were watching the TV as this news helicopter was filming along the coast, just as the big wave from the tsunami was hitting the shores. You could see cars driving away, unaware of how close the wave was to them, but you could see from the speed and direction of the wave that they were about to be swept away.

I don't think I've ever experienced anything like that. To see it like that, in real-time, with it all unfolding in front of me, it was horrific. I was watching people die. I was there watching something horrendous that's going to impact millions of lives, but I was okay at the same time. It was just surreal and something I wouldn't want to experience again. On the actual day, I remember that public transport stopped. You couldn't go anywhere, so I walked the five miles home from the office. It was the strangest vibe. Everyone was out in the street, everyone was walking to get home, so you had all these people out on foot. There was this weird sense of togetherness, though. Japan is quite a reserved nation; they don't really talk to strangers that much. On that day, people were just talking to anyone on the street, just to have that human contact. I think people realized that they'd lived through this era-defining point, and not in a good way, and everyone here remembers where they were. I think it brought a lot of people together, too.

At the end of that year, I left the job and ended up joining a full-time touring band again, but that memory of the earthquake will always live with me.

LEAVING FOR LOVE

GAIL - KUWAIT

I was eighteen when I met the man who became my husband, so I was still quite young. I had a year and a half of happiness with him in Scotland, and then he finished his course and returned to Kuwait. I remember telling my Dad about the relationship and he wasn't sure I should move out there. He warned me that there was a white slave trade there, and that I'd probably end up living in tents with the camels. I loved this guy though and wanted to make that happen, so I pushed on with it.

Back then, it was much harder to get a visa to visit or live in Kuwait, so he had quite a job getting me into the country with him. There were no tourist visas, no student visas, nothing like that. I also didn't hold any higher skills back then, really. Fortunately, there's a big word they have in this country and you learn it from day one, that's wasta. It's an Arabic word and it basically means who and what you know, and the who you know can always help you beat a system or get round something. To get me in, they put me on the books of his Uncle's friend's business, as if I was going to be working for them. It did take

61

eight months, during which time I was losing the will to live, but I got in eventually.

Once I'd booked my flight, my husband gave me instructions on what to say at passport control when I arrived. I was highly nervous about the whole ordeal and spent the flight just frightened about being denied and sent back home. I landed, I got through it, but boy, was my heart beating out of my chest at the time. It was a surreal experience, too. I was surrounded by people in national dress, the landscape was just yellow sand and desert for miles, and it was a real culture shock for me. Those first months I spent there; it was really hard. I didn't have a job, didn't have a car, didn't have friends, and it was one of the hottest places on earth. I'd spend most of the day waiting in the apartment for my husband to get home, then hoping we'd go out for something to eat. It made me feel homesick at times, despite being happy that I was with him. I was really missing home and eventually I just said I couldn't do it anymore, so I flew back to Scotland and lived with my father again.

After spending some time in Baltimore in America, as my husband had been accepted on a course out there, I agreed to give Kuwait another go. This time, I got myself a job, met more people, and got more involved in life. It made a huge difference, it really did. I also started finding things I loved about the country. Okay, it was a bit of a concrete jungle back then and not as glamorous as today, but I do sometimes miss those old days. You'd have these underground basement shops where you'd be able to get cheap clothes, buy houseware that wasn't as expensive, that sort of thing. Dress shops were harder for me though, as it was more Arabic dress styles that they'd sell. What we used to do though was to follow the Kuwaiti women and go down to the material shops. When I used to go home, I'd rip all the pages out of my Mum's catalogues in the style I'd like, then when I got back to Kuwait, I used to get the tailors to measure me. There were tonnes of tailors, absolutely tonnes of them. They'd measure you up, give you a cup of tea or a juice, and you'd then get a made to measure outfit afterwards. When I went back home to the UK after that, people would ask me where I'd get the clothes from. I miss that, that was really fun. After a while, BHS and all these British shops would arrive, and it wasn't really the same again.

One thing that was really difficult for me, though, was that I found out my soon to be husband was originally in an arranged marriage He hadn't really told me about it, so it was a bit of a shock. It turns out he was married to his first cousin and they'd had a child, but he explained that he really shouldn't have done it and was deeply unhappy about it all. He eventually got divorced, which I was adamant about if he wanted to be with me, but his family blamed me for that. I was the white witch from the west that had possessed him and poisoned his tea to make him attracted to me. It was pretty tough. They really didn't want anything to do with me, and that lasted for almost ten years. By that stage, I'd had two children, and my husband was taking them round to see his family without me. At the time, I couldn't understand that, and it really caused me a lot of stress in my relationship. After spending so long in this culture and understanding the family dynamic, I get it now and understand why my husband did that. I respect it now, I just didn't then. After a while though, his mother asked to meet me, and I've built the relationship up from there. Now, the family love me, and I love them. I love his Mum to bits, she's like another mother to me, she's a great woman. They just realized who I was and that I wasn't a threat to anyone.

Initially, when I was working and the kids were growing up, I felt like I'd end up going back to the UK. That changed five years ago though, as I ended up getting diagnosed with breast cancer. With my husband's role in the forces, they were ready to send me anywhere in the world. I stayed here though as, even though the cancer building looks a bit tatty, it's great. The doctors are great, they treat me well, they get me the drugs I need. It's definitely shifted things a bit. I have to get treatment every few weeks now as it's metastasized. If I do go back to England, it's more for little trips. That's really changed things a bit, and it's just a way of life now.

Hey, I'm still here and I'm still plodding on. It's not the end of the world actually, is it? I don't know how much longer I'll be here for, but I just keep going. What I've learned through all of this is that you live for the day, you live in the present, and that's it. Just take each day as if it could be your last, but just enjoy it.

GLYNN – USA

I love telling this story, it's always a good conversation piece. Back in June 1996, I was at a birthday party for my buddy, a few of us got a little drunk, and one of them stayed round at my house. We had the internet back then. It wasn't much, just AOL, but I was showing him how to use chatrooms. When signing up I wanted to use my own name, but that wasn't available, and it started suggesting I added numbers. I didn't want that; I just wanted my name. So, I then just randomly typed on the keyboard and up popped WOLORF, which meant absolutely nothing, but it got me in. So, we went to a US chat room and we were just messing around, when suddenly I got a private message from someone. She apparently liked wolves, saw my screen name and confused it for the animal, and sent me a message. It turns out she was showing her sister how to use the internet, and back in England I was showing my buddy how to use the internet. And we just met in the middle.

We started exchanging emails from there, sending each other mixtapes with letters and pictures through the post, though our music tastes didn't really match up. She was really into early '90s grunge, so bands like Pearl Jam and Nirvana, and I was really into dance music. I'd be down the '70s throwback club in Watford, that was me. We were then in contact with each other every single day for six months before we met. The first thing I'd do when I got home, was quickly dial up the internet, log on, and get the email from her. I looked forward to that every day, I really did. I had a phone line put in after three months, so I didn't have to wait for others to finish on the phone, which was pretty cool. It showed me that my Dad thought it was important and was happy with the idea, too. Then, after six months, I decided to fly out there and meet her.

It was Christmas when we met, and it was brilliant. For me, my family was in turmoil back then and I wasn't fazed by the idea of going to meet her and her family. I arrived, we hugged, and it felt like we'd known each other for years. In fact, her friend, who'd driven her to the airport, said the same thing. He was like, 'Holy crap, it's like you aren't strangers at all.' At first, we didn't want her family and friends to know we'd met online, as it was rare back then, so we concocted this story that I went to college in the US for a semester and that's where we met. The story lasted for around forty-five minutes, as one of her friends arrived, knocked on the door, and said, 'Oh, I guess this must be Glynn.' We couldn't hide it for very long. From then on though, it was clear to us both that we should be together.

One of the reasons we decided I'd move to the US is that my wife's mother had cancer, and she was very sick. In my eyes, I thought there was no way I was going to pull my wife away from her sick mother. It made the decision far easier for me, it just made sense. We set the wedding date a year in advance, which showed to everyone that we were serious and weren't rushing into anything. We then went through the rules and realized that I couldn't move over more than ninety days before the wedding day, so those last few months ended up being a rush. My wife did do most of the organizing with her mother, which I was thankful for.

We went to Florida on our honeymoon, as I wasn't allowed to leave the country. We were at Disney, got back to our room and found a voicemail informing my wife that she'd been fired. On a voicemail. It wasn't even in person. The following night, we went back to our room and found a note to ask us to see the manager. We walked down there and found out that a maid had been raped in our room, so we had to vacate the room because it was now a crime scene. Life has thrown us curveballs like this, but as I always say to my wife, 'We'll just get through these problems, learn from them, get stronger from them, and go again.' People at work always say that a grey cloud hangs over me, yet I remain so calm, happy, and chilled. This is what life does, though. You deal with it, you find a way, and you keep going. We still had a good time; we just have some crazy memories from it.

That whole period, to the wedding and the next three months, was just one pure adrenaline rush. It was a blur, but I've never once thought I'd made a mistake or didn't want to be there. I remember going into New York City for the first time and thinking, 'What the hell? I'm living here now? I'm living in New York?' We spent New Year's Eve in Times Square with the ball dropping and all that. Even twenty-three years later, when I go into the city for tax conferences and so on, I still walk down to Times Square, I wander down Fifth Avenue, I go and see the Empire State Building. It's an amazing city. Every year, we take the family into the city to see the Christmas decorations, the lights, go for dinner and see a show, maybe see the Rockettes who play every Christmas.

How many things could have happened or could have been different over the years, though? A few months before meeting Chrissy online, I turned down a job opportunity in Central London. Perhaps, taking that job would've changed the course of my life and maybe I'd have never met this amazing woman. The circumstances in which we met, both being in the same chat room, for the same reasons, at the exact same time, and messaging each other by chance? If there was a chance of fate ever being real in life, that was it for me. I don't regret any decisions, because if I'd have changed one single thing, this might not have happened. I've met my best friend. I've met my buddy. Twenty-four years on, and if anything, we're getting closer. Everything that happened, it happened for a reason.

AMANDA - NETHERLANDS

I owned a flat in Watford at the time, so I sold that and most of my belongings. I then put what I had left on a trailer we borrowed from the Dutch police and caught a night boat across to the Netherlands. By the time I moved, I'd only been in the relationship for nine months, but it just felt different to any others I'd had before. The idea of moving over to be with him, that just made total sense to me. What helped was that my brother had already set a precedent, having met his wife on the internet and then moving across to New York to be with her. He'd already laid the groundwork, as it were. It meant no one was really surprised when I came in with my news, which helped.

We initially stayed at my Dutch partner's family home, with his mum and his sister. That was weird for me and I did struggle with it at times. I'd already made that break myself and left home, and I was now not only back into a family environment, but this time they were Dutch. I was suddenly thrown into a world where nothing was familiar. I'd done language prep before I moved over, but the family consciously spoke very little English to me, and I couldn't always follow what was happening. It could be quite humiliating at times, too. We stayed for two months with them, during which time I found a job in an English-speaking environment. So, during the day I spoke English, and I then went back into that Dutch environment after work. That was hard, but they forced me to speak the language, which really helped me pick it up. Cruel to be kind springs to mind.

I was homesick at times. I do remember going through a phase of thinking, 'Everything here sucks, everything in England is so much better', too. I'd also constantly question why the Dutch weren't doing things more like the English. While I was going through that, I had absolutely no idea that this was completely normal for people in new countries. It was only when I started a writing career, looking into culture shock and ex-pat blues, that I realised it was just a phase and it would disappear. Sure enough, I went over into the acceptance phase and now I'm completely the opposite; I think the Dutch do it better.

One of the turning points for me, was meeting up with an ex-pat group. It was one of the most horrific experiences I ever had; it was miserable. The group all had Dutch partners and there wasn't a single positive thing going on in the room that night. Some people had just arrived in the Netherlands, others had been here years, but everyone was extremely negative about their experiences of being here. When you started delving into it, they just didn't have much going on outside of their relationships. Their only real social interactions, beyond their Dutch partner, were with their friends and family back in England, Wales, Scotland, or wherever else they came from. They'd complain that they couldn't make Dutch friends, but they weren't willing to learn the language. They were stuck in the lowest point of the culture shock curve and couldn't clamber out. That was a real tipping point for me. I realized I didn't need to be stuck in that world with that negativity. I needed to be more involved with the area, with the local people, with the country I was living in. If you're going to move to another country, and you want to make roots and stay there, you do need to integrate. You need to learn the language; you need to accept the way that things are done. It doesn't mean you have to agree with it all, but it's certainly not going to change just for you.

I think becoming a mother accelerated my integration, if I'm honest. Getting involved in pre-school and then primary school, throwing myself into that school life, helping with things like reading with children, volunteering in the class, that made a big difference. I just started naturally having more contact with local people, talking to the other parents in Dutch. But even after twenty years here, I still can't get away with passing for a local. No one speaks to me in English anymore, but they can hear I'm not Dutch and can't quite put their finger on where I'm from. When we moved to this village a few years ago, the rumours about an English woman were in full flow before I met anyone. People were curious, full of questions: 'Why are you here? How long have you been in the Netherlands? Do you like it? What are the differences between here and England?' I see the questions as a positive thing, an icebreaker that really helps to start conversations.

I feel more Dutch than British these days. I've had Dutch nationality since 2016 and I'm not planning to renew my British passport next year. I've come to the point where I feel weird when I'm back in England. It takes me a while to adjust when I'm there, to remember I used to live there. I can't envision myself ever living back there. In fact, I can't even remember the last time I wished I was living back in the UK.

JAMES – JAPAN

I've always had an interest in Japanese things, and in fact a lot of what I liked as a kid originated in Japan without me realizing. Things like Pokémon and Dragonball for example. Then I'd watch Takeshi's Castle, which I'm sure you've seen. It's funny, that show's actually from the '80s but was just being shown on countless re-runs in the UK when I was in school. When you mention it to the younger people here, they have absolutely no idea what you're talking about. I'm also a musician, and I really like Japanese artists like X Japan, Yellow Magic Orchestra, Ryuichi Sakamoto, people like that. I'm not finished there, either, as I like films, and my friends and I used to watch lots of Japanese films back at university. We particularly liked Kurasawa's films, a director who is pretty well known outside of Asia, too. So, when I met a Japanese lady in Leeds, and later married her, it wasn't a huge surprise to my close family. In fact, my Mum always said she knew that I'd end up here one day.

After we got married, we had a choice. Either my wife could get a visa for the UK or I could get a visa in Japan. We started the process of getting her a visa in the UK and it was incredibly stressful and incredibly expensive. So, we started looking at Japan and it was easier and cheaper, oddly enough. With that in mind, it just sounded like a pretty good excuse to set up operations here. I'd only been to Japan once before; we went last year to meet my wife's family, so they could check that I was alright before we got married, really. We only came for six days, which in hindsight was far too short. So, the idea of living here, being surrounded by all these things I'm interested in, that was definitely exciting.

It's not as different here as people make it out to be, though. People talk about how it's going to blow your mind, that it's going to be a completely different experience, and that I'd feel like an alien here. But that's not really been my experience. There are little differences, but I haven't found any massive obstacles. It's often from people who haven't actually been here, too. One difference I have found is people's attitude to work. They work too hard here. I was looking at jobs to apply for and I noticed that the list of holidays you get are the usual seasonal ones, but then you only get six days personal holiday per year. Then, when I read underneath it said that they recommend you use these when you are sick. That's not great, is it? So, I do think the work ethic is a bit of a problem here. People can take work too seriously; they'll dedicate their lives to it and shun time with their families. My wife is always thinking about her work, she's worried about upsetting people or annoying them and seems scared of being sick. Studies have shown that working too hard is inefficient, though. Apparently, productivity can be increased by twenty percent if you only work four days a week. So, it's not even beneficial for people to work so hard.

When you go out here, you notice that a lot of people do get drunk and try to have a good time. The big difference is that it's never in an aggressive way like it can be back in England. You'll see them walking home in a zig-zag fashion, talking to random people, and generally acting a little sleepy. They'll also try to speak English more when drunk. They're never threatening, though. I think that's because there's a culture of not inconveniencing people, which I like. I think there's a fear of shame here too, which is a double-edged sword. I get the impression that if you did get arrested or sentenced to prison, you'd have a mark of shame on you forever. It's not just crime, though. It can apply to everyday situations, like something simple such as trying to speak English with you. They're scared of making a mistake, and it leads to them coming across as very shy and very reserved. Little mistakes, they're a bigger thing here for people. I think that's a big part of why there's so little crime here in Japan, especially petty crimes. It's just not worth the social costs to nick some alcohol or a chocolate bar from a shop. In the UK, people can be far easier going about things. The downside to that is the lack of social deterrent and the lack of shame for some of the things you see people doing or hear people saying.

We haven't set a time limit for being here in Japan, to be honest. I'm not the sort of person who plans too far ahead, I tend to wing it a bit. I do want to go back to the UK at some point, though. Whether that's in two years or twenty years, we'll have to see. It's not necessarily the country itself that I want to return to. It's more the friends and family there that I'd like to be around again.

BELINDA - USA & GERMANY

I totally tanked my A-levels, although I tried so hard. It ended up being an awful year for me. Instead of studying German at University, I ended up doing European Business Studies, which was effectively a useless qualification. It was a sandwich course though, so it was six months in college and six months in industry, and you repeated that for three years. During my second year, I was working as a tour guide in this beautiful German town called Traben-Trarbach in the Mosel valley, a real fairy-tale place. While working, I noticed a lot of Americans wandering around and, in my naivety, wondered why so many of them had short haircuts. I just didn't pick up on the theme at first. Anyway, in my last weekend in the town at the end of a six-month stint there, I ended up meeting my future husband, who was stationed over there with the US Air Force.

I didn't think much about him at first and headed back to college in the UK. He completely wooed me though, so much that I spent much of my vacation time going back and forth to Germany to see him. That culminated in the two of us getting married once he was assigned to England, and we lived together for four years in RAF Lakenheath. I was twenty-two, thought I was well travelled, thought I was worldly, but really, I was just extremely impulsive and didn't think anything through. I honestly thought I was invincible and that everything would be fine. When I was 25 and pregnant, he got ordered back to the United States and that was it. I said a tearful goodbye to my family, not really grasping this was permanent, and off we went.

Our relationship was built around a case of opposites attract, really. He was American. I was English. Wasn't this all fun, let's move, let's do it, this is going to be great. Except it wasn't. I went from Bury St Edmunds to this tiny little hick town in South Georgia. He'd spent the last ten years out of the country and was thrilled to be back, whereas the move just left me with this huge culture shock. I was pregnant with my first child and very hormonal, and nothing was working for me. I quickly became very depressed. I didn't know anyone, I couldn't drive as I was too big to fit behind the steering wheel, and I was effectively a prisoner inside this house. It felt like solitary confinement, and I was unbearably lonely, compounded by the fact that our marriage was very empty. That was pretty much my existence for two years. I would spend time back in the UK and whenever it came to getting back on the plane, I'd always question why I was going back We weren't happily married, and he could never really empathise or understand my feelings. He just couldn't relate to what I was going through. But when you have children, it's no longer just about you.

When my daughter was a year old, I got a part time job at a department store and that really helped me. I met a group of English wives who were in the same boat, too, and life just totally turned around. It was so much brighter and so much cheerier. A group of us got together once a week, and we all had children around the same age, so we instantly had something to talk about. It was my saving grace, really. We were all in the same situations, but we all gradually got deployed to other sites and had to say our goodbyes. I think that's the hardest thing about being married to someone in the forces. As soon as you get settled and find your niche, then it's time to move on. Just as I'd finally found my own piece of home there, we were ordered to New Mexico and I had to leave all of that behind.

I had three children by the time I decided to go to college, just to give myself more options. The thing is, I was busy being a wife and a mum and I had no idea how to operate newer computers or what "windows" were all about. Everyone was suddenly talking about the internet and e-mails, and I had absolutely no idea what was going on. So, I decided that if I ever wanted a job again, I needed to get re-educated. I took some basic classes and started a part-time job. I suddenly felt like I was developing as a person, getting braver and branching out, and really clawing my way back into the real world. After getting a full-time job from there, both my outlook and my personal life changed. We finally got divorced, I met a new guy pretty quickly, and stayed in New Mexico. Unfortunately, that marriage unravelled within a year, and I was a single Mum in a state where I had no family.

America is a brutal place to be a struggling single parent. It's a country founded around the haves and have-nots, and it might be billed as the land of the free and of great opportunities, but that's never really worked out for me. And here I was, single, with three children, and no idea what to do about it. I wasn't going crawling back to my parents in England and living in some council house, though. I'd also have a massive custody battle on my hands if I tried to take the children out of the country, so that wasn't an option. I ended up moving to Wisconsin, where my ex-husband was from, and moving my three children into his mother's house, as strange as that sounds. She was wonderful to me and without her I would not have made it.

I really, really struggled at times. It was a really dark decade for me, and I absolutely hated living outside of England by then. I missed my family and everything that had been comfortable about home, even though going back would have been a huge struggle and admitting that I had failed. It felt like the further away I was in miles, the harder it was psychologically. I also felt that, in order to fit in, I had to try and lose some of my personality and who I fundamentally was, and that's a really sad process. Americans don't understand or embrace sarcasm and the English style of humour very well and I had to adapt so much just to make myself understood in the way I said things, so you go into survival mode and start denying those parts of your personality. I've always really struggled with that, having to outwardly change my personality to just be accepted and understood.

After being in the country for almost 30 years, I feel fortunate that I have three great children who are doing very well. I also now have a wonderful husband, and I'm enjoying life in Green Bay. It's been a hard route here, though. My life so far, which I chose for myself I should add, is a cautionary tale for others. It's a look before you leap type tale, really. Would I do it all again? No, I wouldn't. I wish I'd thought things through carefully and had a backup plan at the time. If you can take one thing from what I've told you, is don't get stuck in a place where you have nothing to fall back on and no escape route. Living abroad is only glamourous until things go badly wrong and there is no way out.

JOHN - USA

I was working in social care in Carlisle, initially as a carer and then I moved into the office and started handling the schedules and staffing. Everyone was on zero-hours contracts at the time, as that's how social care works in England, so it was quite frustrating. After that, I became a live call monitor, so I was doing lots of reporting, meeting the council, that sort of thing. It sounds dull, doesn't it? I can't lie, it was pretty dull. Unfortunately, around the time I met my wife online, the rest of my life became a little more dramatic around me.

For a start, Carlisle flooded for the second time in ten years and left my house under about six feet of water. It was mad. I went away for the weekend on the Friday afternoon in shorts and t-shirt as the weather was beautiful. Then on the Saturday, it flooded, and my house was rendered completely unliveable, just hours later. As result, I ended up moving in with my Mum. Sadly, my stepdad, her husband, became seriously ill while I was there, with cancer spreading throughout his body, and he died within two months. It left my Mum close to a nervous breakdown and she decided she couldn't stay in that house, instead moving over to Newcastle with my brother for a fresh start. My head was all over the place at the time, as you can imagine. Not only had I lost my own home, but the rest of my family had move away and I was stuck in Carlisle on my own.

The story of how I actually met my wife from there, that always makes me laugh. We met on Tinder; I'll be honest. The thing is, I didn't have my location set to fucking Chicago at the time. It showed up that this person, Cindy, was thirty miles away and we just started chatting. I'm just there trying out all my best lines, you know, and then I click on her profile and it says, 'Cindy lives 5,000 miles away.' That was a surprise. Apparently, she had this passport feature turned on, something I was completely unaware of. It normally talks about hot singles in your area, right? Well, it turns out you can use this passport feature if you're going on holiday, helping you match with local people there. She said she was sick of guys in the Midwest, so just tried England for fun. Carlisle would've been a weird place to pick though, right? Anyway, we just carried on chatting, exchanged WhatsApp details, starting skyping on a weekly basis, and then I deleted my Tinder and it went from there. A modern love story, hey?

Cindy hadn't been to Europe before meeting me, in fact she didn't even have a passport at first, and I'd never been to America, either. She was really keen to come to Europe first though, so we planned this trip to Carlisle of all places. Naturally Carlisle Castle is one of the first places you want to see, right? We then planned to go up to Scotland, down to London, and then across to Paris, as most Americans love the thought of going to Paris. When she arrived, we just had this instant chemistry between us. There were no awkward silences or anything, we just hit it off. To this day, four years later, we've never really argued either. That does surprise me at times, as I'm dead sarcastic and often a bit of a dickhead. She doesn't seem to mind that too much, fortunately.

With the trip ending in Paris, we were on a boat trip on the river, just sitting at the back of the boat on this beautiful day. It was there that she turned to me and goes, 'I think I want to marry you.' It hadn't really crossed my mind; I was just enjoying that week. I hadn't thought ahead, I had no five- or ten-year plans at that stage. She explained that she was just having a really lovely time, that we got on, and she wasn't wrong either. It did take me by surprise, admittedly, but I wasn't against the idea at all. She then flew home from Paris, and from there we started looking at our options. We decided it was best if I fly out to the States too, just to see if I was comfortable with the idea. So, I went over for Thanksgiving and met her family, her friends, and her dog. It was all really nice, this welcoming family environment, and I had a great time. So that was it, I was moving to America.

We still talk about it, but realistically, if I didn't have to emigrate, then we wouldn't be married at this stage. The thing is, I didn't earn enough money, working in the care section, to allow Cindy to move to the UK. On the other hand, Cindy earned relatively good money in the US and could support my visa process. So, I became a ninety-day fiancé. It's a big thing here, especially as there's this appalling TV show about it. The idea is that you must get married within ninety days of arriving in the country in order to get your K-1 visa. If you don't, you'll have to leave, or risk being deported. It's not often as straight forward as that, but we didn't take any risks and got married at the courthouse after sixty days. We had planned a bigger wedding, but without me being able to work, the costs were just too high. What then happens, is that my wife is essentially signing to take responsibility for me. I can't claim any state benefits and I'm not entitled to anything from the government, that's on the person signing for you. So, if we get divorced and I've mugged her off and she gets catfished, that's her bad luck. She'd then have to pay for me for the next ten years. That's how the government sees it, and it does that to protect itself from people sneaking into the country, claiming a green card, and then claiming benefits. Fortunately for Cindy, I have no intention of doing that.

EMMA – MEXICO

Everyone in England has this impression that Mexico is just full of drug deals, cartels, and illegal activity. Yet, the first time I came here, I didn't see anything wrong. I felt safe, really. I'll admit that when we then moved out; I was still really worried about security in general. We moved to Michoacán, and that's a state that's had a lot of issues with the drug cartels, and that was one of my first concerns. So far though, it's nothing like the stereotypes that people talk about back home. My parents were still worried, for sure. I'm the first one in my extended family to go abroad, and it's not like Mexico is a common route for people, is it? The location definitely surprises people. I'm sure people consider Spain quite often, but Mexico? Probably not.

This all came about because I met my now fiancé when we were studying for our PhDs in musical composition at Manchester University. He's from Mexico City originally, and when we finished our studies, he got the opportunity to do a post-doctorate back in his home city. My family and friends knew that this move was on the cards for a while, and whenever anyone met us, they'd ask us whether we'd move to Mexico in future. The immigrations calls had become quite tough in the UK, so the chance of me leaving were always pretty high if I wanted to keep this relationship going. Even if you've studied at a PhD level in England, there's no guarantee that you can stay. So, we knew that it would be difficult for us. In Mexico on the other hand, it was far easier for me to move here. Once you're married, there really aren't any conditions, either.

Leaving For Love

I spent the first eighteen months between the two countries, and I did find that difficult. I was then offered a job at the same university as my fiancé, so I'm now a lecturer in Music and Artistic Technology here in Morelia, Michoacán. Working at a university in this country, I actually find the workload far more than back home. In English university, you tend to have multiple lecturers, multiple teachers, and far more independent study. Whereas here, you lead the whole course by yourself and I'm then responsible for quite a few students on my own. I'm also left to my own devices here and that initially seemed a little overwhelming. You design your own courses from scratch and you're responsible for the evaluations and the feedback, too. I think the students expect a lot more from the lecturers, too. Here, they still treat it more like school. So, I'm expected to help more, to communicate more. Whereas the universities in England, you're expected to go off on your own. Now I've got used to this, I really enjoy it. You get to treat the students more as individuals, you can give them better quality teaching, and you can really improve yourself as a teacher.

As I said earlier, I think the stereotypes about this country are massively unfair. Of course, there is crime and there are rural areas where people do live in bad conditions, but show me a country where that's not an issue? In many ways, it's a very modern country. In Mexico City, the capital, you could be in any other modern city at times. It has the modern skyscrapers, the huge commercial centres, and a reliable metro system. So, the stereotypes about it being riddled with crime, that it's disorganized, that they're a country of people looking to break into America, I think they're really unfair. I also find that people don't talk about Donald Trump and his wall here, especially in this city. They're far more interested in Mexican politics and what happens in their country. Admittedly that might be different in some of the more rural areas, where you have people living in poverty and with limited opportunities, but it's definitely not the majority of the country like it's portrayed. It's a shame that people can only see that side of it at times. Now that I've been here a few years, I've realized that I was overly worried about my security. There are good people here, there's bad people, but I sometimes feel far safer here than I did back home in Manchester.

I think this move has done me a lot of good, really. I feel I've learned a lot here. It's also opened my eyes a lot, especially as I'd only lived in one place prior to this. I really enjoy the lifestyle here, the focus on traditional values and families, and the food. In fact, I really, really love the food. I love being able to go to the market and get really fresh fruit and vegetables. It's meant that I've lost a fair bit of weight without really trying, too.

This is a really nice place to live, all my neighbours are really friendly and supportive, it's good.

REBECCA - USA & GERMANY

At the time we met online, I was studying in Nottingham and the American guy who's now my husband, he was deployed in Kosovo. We met on this art website, as we're both amateur photographers and keen writers, and we bonded there. It's a little embarrassing to talk about now, but you know how it goes. This was back in 2006 and meeting someone online wasn't as common. Sure, you had paid dating websites, but you definitely didn't have all the apps you can use today. Anyway, he came across to visit me when he was on leave and that was it, we were together. It just really worked between us. He proposed to me during those two weeks, I said yes, and he then had to go back to Kosovo. It was a bit of a whirlwind, as you can imagine. I'd only known him for six months by then, but it felt right to me and I was really happy. We were both single before that, we didn't have children, and we were both twenty-one. So, I just remember thinking, 'What's the worst that could happen here?'

At the time he proposed, we did talk about our options. The way we saw it, we had two choices. Either wait for him to be finished with the army, so he could live in England, or I had to move to America. So, I ended up moving. To me, that was the only real option, I didn't want to wait years to see how it all played out. It was exciting, I wasn't doing anything else, well, aside from my degree but I wasn't enjoying that, and I just didn't want to miss out on something like this. I was very much in love and carried away with it all. Admittedly not many people leave in the middle of their degree, marry someone in the army, and move to another country, but I didn't see why that shouldn't happen to me. Looking back as an adult, it doesn't seem like a sensible idea, sure, but it has worked out. My parents must've been concerned, but they met him, liked him, and my Mum was fully on board with my idea. She thought if I hated it, the worse that could happen was that I'd just move back home again. It wasn't that big a deal, as such.

We moved to Texas initially, and for those first two years I didn't go back to England once. It's not that I didn't want to, we were just young and didn't have the money to spend on international travel. In hindsight, I suppose, it was a rough start for me. I wasn't able to work while I was waiting for my green card and I also couldn't drive, so at times I felt a little isolated and alone. I also got pregnant with my son while we were there, and being away from my Mum at that time, that was difficult. It wasn't really part of the big plan for us at the time, either. It's not that we weren't thrilled, we had just never mapped out what we wanted. We both took things as they come, and still do today, but I can't pretend it was all easy for me. I was sticking it out for love partly, but I'm also not the type of person who just easily gives up, so I trusted in it all and hoped we'd eventually come out the other side. We eventually did, though.

The thing with being married to someone in the army, and

I'm sure I'm not the first person to say this, is that you get used to relocating. My husband ended up being posted to Heidelberg in Germany, so we moved back to Europe. It was a great experience, though. I loved living there. My son was young, and the Germans love kids, so that really worked for us. And living in a European city after being in Texas, that was great. We chose to live closer to town, to get involved in the local supermarkets and the shops, and I'm really happy we did that. A few of the Americans wondered how we coped, and we would still get a few staples on base, but I think throwing ourselves into it was the best idea. We ended up living there for four years, after which my husband left the army and we moved back to his hometown, a place near Chicago.

Living in America, it's certainly been interesting. I'm self-employed here, and do some communications, marketing, and web development for small businesses. You'll find that people are thrilled to have a British person helping them, too. It seems exciting for them. I think that's because British people are exotic enough to Americans, but without being scary or unfamiliar to them. And in general, I've found the people here to be very nice. I've come across so many wonderful, warm, welcoming people. It seems to counter what you'll often see on TV about Americans, that they're this angry and entitled country. They do have this American exceptionalism at times and think that they're bigger and better than the rest of the world, but you just need to look at their healthcare or their politics to see that it's not the case. Aside from that, you do have plenty of normal, nice, rational people living here. It's always felt very welcoming to me. I'll get the odd joke on July 4th, but I'll just meet that with a heavy dose of sarcasm, and it'll fly completely over their heads. It'll make me laugh, though.

CHASING DREAMS

SAM – USA

I didn't go through the main drama schools in London, so I was finding it hard to get in front of any decent casting directors back there. I had no big TV credits or anything like that, and that can really make a difference. I managed to find myself a relatively decent manager and agent though, and he was getting me auditions for self-tapes, where you film yourself doing a scene, for roles in Los Angeles and Hollywood. It got to the point where I was working hard to get somewhere in London, but getting nowhere, so I thought I'd be better off putting my energies into California and seeing what happens. I made a rough plan to come out here by myself for pilot season, which is traditionally the first few months of the year, and just thought I'd see what I could achieve.

I originally booked my flights for a ninety-day stay, but I ended up getting everything done in that first two months and returned to the UK earlier to start the visa process. The main goal was to find a local agent, someone on the ground there who could sponsor me, find me job offers, put their name to me, that sort of thing. That worked out pretty well and I met some cool people. I went for an audition, too, and I booked this cheesy web series that ended up having some relative success and gained a load of views, which helped with my visa application. I had to pay a huge amount for that whole process though, lawyer included, and that felt pretty painful at the time. The process also took almost two years, so it definitely wasn't an instant Hollywood success story for me.

I just had this really strong drive to move to LA, especially once I'd been there. For me, when I was in London, I knew one other actor and I felt so far away from acting as a profession. When I came to LA, everyone here is either part of the industry or knows someone in the industry. I was getting invited to Q&As or screenings with big directors and actors and it felt incredible. It all felt right here. It felt tangible. Just having the experience of being closer to it, even though I was still a million miles away, was still incredible. I wasn't sure how I was going to navigate everything, but I thought I'd just take it one step at a time, as I've always done. I set an end goal and then just started chipping away at it slowly, slowly. I was always very optimistic about it, even when there were times when it was extremely hard, seemingly impossible, to get the visa done. I just had to put it to one side and chip away at it. The thing with LA is, there's a lot of opportunities but there are a lot more people too. It's had its difficulties, but at the same time I've met amazing people here, people who've taught me a lot and inspired me, and I've met some incredible friends. I still think I've got more opportunities here; in fact, I can almost guarantee it compared to London.

The biggest thing that I've landed is a Christmas movie that was filmed in Canada. It was an amazing experience, getting to go there for three weeks and film. Looking back, I feel like I could've given a better performance, maybe even a thousand percent better, but I gave the best I could at the time and learned a lot from it. Luckily, I have some good friends and a good mentor here, and they'll often remind me that I need to appreciate all these opportunities. They'll never blow smoke up my arse, but they'll also pull me away from being negative and not celebrating my achievements. They're good like that, and I think it's important to have people like that around you in this profession. If I was on my own, I'd have been too critical and not have taken it all in. There are so many actors around the world that would kill to have that role and to be a lead in any film, especially one that was properly made and had an actual run, so I should be grateful for that. That opportunity, for some people anyway, is their dream, and I was living it. I have to be super appreciative of that. It was a huge opportunity and now I have a TV movie to my name. It's hard not to be critical, though. It's a human thing, but it's compounded being British, I think. We're more self-critical from what I've seen, it's just part of our culture in so many ways.

There's nothing particularly glamorous about auditions. Most of the time you don't book anything from them. There are a million reasons why you might not get the job, sometimes it's already gone and they're just doing the auditions as a formality. There are times when you can be perfect for a part, and they like you, but there's someone else better. It's a numbers game and there's so much out of your control. All you can control, is what you brought and how much you contributed. I just try to work on myself as much as possible, and that's the case whether I get a part of not, really. Acting is like an instrument, you need to keep practicing it, keep trying new things, be willing to be vulnerable and open to criticism. It's certainly not easy, especially showing your emotions, you know. As boys we're told not to cry. We're constantly encouraged to repress our emotions, but that's the opposite of what you need to do with acting. You need to allow your emotions to come out, which is something I'm always working at.

I'm here in Hollywood, working as an actor, as there's nothing else I want to do. There's a drive within me that takes me down this path. If I thought I could let it go and do something else, I probably would. It's such a challenging path to go down, and you know it's going to be painful, but you do it anyway. I'll always see this experience, wherever it takes me, as an achievement. I actually went to live in another country, moved my whole life here, to try and achieve a dream. If that's the least, I gave it my all and went for what I wanted and gained so much life and experience from it.

CHRISTINE – TURKEY

I met my husband while working as a mini-cab driver in London. We got married but he didn't like me working the cabs at night, you see, so I started picking up packages instead. One day, I was sent on a long journey and I was starving. I picked up this package from some industrial estate and I stopped at a burger van for something to eat. I had a bacon sandwich from them, and it was absolutely delicious. Proper bacon sandwich, just the way I like it. The following day, I was sent on another long journey to pick up a package from an industrial estate. My mouth was watering from the bacon sandwich the day before, so this time I stopped at another van and picked up two more. They were disgusting, though, and I thought I could do much better than that. I relayed this story about the bacon sandwiches to my husband when I got back and told him I'd like to run my own van. He liked the idea, we looked into it, and it all went from there.

Because I'd worked a lot in the Epsom Downs area, I knew a lot about the derby and how food vans went down a treat there. Getting into burger vans isn't as easy as people think, though, so it was no guarantee that we could make that work. We agreed that if we could get a spot at the derby, then we'd go hell-for-leather for it. We got it, it went great, and we then spent the next twenty years in London running burger vans. We'd work twenty-four seven at times, but we eventually got a pitch outside a nightclub in Croydon and business was great. By the time we got divorced, we had about four different burger vans. I kept that nightclub spot, and he kept the others.

I was coming up to an age where I wanted to do something more after that. I'd hit a crossroads in my life, as it were. I just knew that I wanted to go somewhere else, maybe to retire somewhere in the sun. So, I sold my business, sold my house, and I was living in a rented apartment for a year. I gave myself that year to work out what to do with my life, basically. Then, in the local paper one weekend there was an advert for homes in Turkey and I instantly loved the idea of it. I got all excited, went down to this exhibition, but it was just a room in a hotel with posters of Spain and Turkey on the walls. There were a few women in there and I told them I was only interested in Turkey, so that instantly cut down my options. A friend of mine had recently bought an apartment in Spain you see, and she'd bought it off-plan a few years earlier. I went out there with her for a holiday and I hated the place. This brand-new apartment, it'd only been finished a month before, it was grey and looked like Nelson Mandela House in Peckham. There was rubbish downstairs, there was graffiti, there was dirty needles. Once you got inside though, it was quite nice in fairness. She had a view over the pool, too. I couldn't get over how dirty some of the outside was, and that really put me off Spain in general. It had never been a holiday destination for me, in fairness.

Anyway, going back to this exhibition, I thought it was a complete waste of time. This lady took my name and telephone number, just in case, but I wasn't expecting much. Then I got a phone call on the Monday asking if I wanted to go on an inspection trip to Turkey and look at some places. They do that, they do. They'll send you out there, look after you a bit, and try to pitch all these new builds on you. I took them up on the offer and I liked the area, but the rep was with me the whole time trying to put the blinkers on me. I already said that I wasn't interested in off-plan, I'd rather have a re-sell, or something already built. She just took me to building sites though and that was a nightmare. I managed to escape for about half an hour and found loads of estate agents. They were everywhere. I went into this smaller place though and this guy just gave me this little pamphlet and we had a chat. After a few phone calls, including a persuasive one from his Scottish wife, I ended up buying a ready-made apartment from them.

When it came time to move, I was the first person to move into these apartments and there's a funny story there. You see, I know at least twenty different people said they'd sent me new home cards, but I didn't see a single one. The apartments didn't have a name though, so the post just wasn't making it to me. There I was, stamping my feet and having a tantrum at the builder, and they said they'd fix it. I came home one day and there's a big sign on the apartments, it read, 'Christine Apartments', so they'd just stuck my actual name on it. I felt like the bee's knees, there I was with the whole place named after me, until I worked out that it actually wasn't very good. Everyone then knew Christine from Christine Apartments you see, and they thought I was mega rich, that I owned the whole block. I then had these young Turkish toy boys asking me if I had a boyfriend and if I wanted one. Obviously, I said, 'No, thank you very much', just to be clear, but they still thought I was this rich single woman for some time.

I love it here, though. The small block I live in, it's all Turkish people here now. I'm the only Brit, and I'm fairly thankful for that. We don't have a pool or a bar or anything like that, but it also means we don't have that constant gossip, the arguments, the Brits abroad mentality. That's all you hear in those places, just loads of gossip around the pool. We're still invaded by them, though. It's a shame that so many lowlifes come here. You go into the supermarket and you'll see some tart with God knows how many brats in pushchairs, and she's wearing a bikini. While we're more Westernised in this part, it's still a Muslim area. The Brits abroad, they'll go on the buses without their shirts on and in their bikinis and just expect the locals to be fine with that. The Turks are very patient with them and very forgiving, but what's the problem with putting something on and showing some respect? It makes me really angry at times and, to add to that, I don't want to be sat next to some big, sweaty, beer bellied Brit with no shirt on while I'm in my best clothes, do I?

AMIN – BULGARIA

I started my journey through medical school quite young. I started at twenty and I studied for five years in London. I then had some family problems, let's just call them that, and ended up leaving the course. I did start training to be a barrister after that, but I just really missed medicine and decided to give it another shot once my family situation was resolved. I spoke to one of my old tutors and she suggested trying again in another part of Europe. So, I started applying for courses and worked as a chef in the meantime to save up some money. I was offered places in Malta and Bulgaria, but Bulgaria had a dedicated surgical programme, so I decided to go there.

I was very scared. I was expecting an "Enemy at the Gate" type of scene. I arrived in Pleven in February, it was blistering cold, and I was...I was scared. I was very down about it. My friends thought it was fucking mental. They had to Google search where the fuck Bulgaria was, and I'd never been East of the Czech Republic before. The thing is, they knew that I was the type of person who was incredibly dedicated and would go to the end of the earth, literally, to do what I wanted. If a door is open, I'm willing to go there. I just looked at it like I was going to prison, really. I figured some people go to prison for six years and come out with nothing, whereas I'm effectively going to prison for six years and will come out with a medical degree. Then I could go back to the UK and do what I'd always wanted to do. So, that's what I did.

I was in the second cohort to come from the UK and we were about eighty students in all. Most of them were eighteen and nineteen, whereas I was twenty-nine at the time. So, I was the eldest. There were a few others who were twenty-six or twenty-seven. The older ones wanted to do medicine at some point but, through whatever dice that life rolled for them, they couldn't quite do it. The eighteen-year-olds on the other hand, they were the people who didn't get the right A-levels, and they didn't want to wait to apply again, so ended up in Bulgaria, too. In the UK, there's this thing that if you don't jump on the train at the right time, then the door is closed forever and you miss out. People think you must finish college at eighteen, then go straight to University. Finish there at twenty-one. Do a masters. Do a PhD. Get married. Buy a house, etc. And the people who are a year or two years behind, they genuinely see themselves as failures. And you can see it in the way they conduct themselves, like they're lesser. I think because I 'got into medical school' in the first place, I refused to have that mentality. I went there as if I was the Count of Monte Cristo, whereby I exile myself for a bit and then I come back better than I was.

The first year was difficult. I had to learn Bulgarian obviously, as the town I lived in and at the school, no one spoke any English. So, you had to learn very quickly. We got taught Bulgarian twice a week for the first three years, with the course being taught in English. And after those three years, you had to pass the Bulgarian test to go onto the three-year clinical phase. Though we didn't study with the Bulgarians initially, we did spend a lot of time together. My friends did too. We really tried to live in Bulgaria, rather than flying home every few weeks. I feel that if you really engross yourself in a country and its people, you learn it's culture, you learn it's language, then you truly understand the country.

Healthcare in Bulgaria, I think, is excellent. They're not regulated like they are in the UK, so when you become a fully qualified consultant level doctor, you have full autonomy to do what you like. The benefit of that when you live in the community, is that the doctors have the ability to not charge a patient for surgery. If they know the patient really needs the surgery, they can charge them whatever they want. It can be less than the price of the surgery. It could be free. Many a time I've seen doctors do really complex surgeries in return for about five dozen eggs, as the person was a farmer and that's all they could afford. They didn't charge them eggs, obviously, but the patient gave the surgeon eggs as a thank you. They'd bring in a huge crate of eggs, too, so it wasn't just a fig leaf type of payment for them.

The hospitals can look and feel like they've been hit by a war. They are underfunded. Crumbling. They don't have the physical infrastructure. But whatever they lack monetarily, they make up for in integrety. They make up for in how good the doctors and physicians are. They are amazing. I've seen someone do a pericardiocentesis, which is a procedure where you put a needle between the sac that covers your heart and when that fills up with fluid for whatever reason, it stops it from expanding and beating and the patient will die. So, you need to put a needle in and suck that fluid out. In the UK that's done with an ultrasound, but in Bulgaria they have mastered and perfected the ability to do it just by palpation, so tapping on your chest and listening to it with a stethoscope. I've seen doctors do that procedure with nothing but a needle and a stethoscope. That is amazing clinical ability. They really stick to their acumen. They're able to do things that our doctors are incapable of doing as they're busy relying on machines and they're relying on the idea of the gold standard. We don't allow people to practice like they do in Bulgaria. The thing is, I'm sure anyone coming from the UK to a Bulgarian hospital would probably think they were going to die, just by looking at the place and jumping to assumptions. That's not the case and never will be. They don't look pretty, but they get the job done.

By the end of the six years, you know, I started to have Stockholm Syndrome and didn't want to leave. It was difficult learning Bulgarian, it was difficult living in a foreign land without family or friends, it was difficult understanding the alphabetic, as it's in Cyrillic for god's sake. But if you stop changing and stop growing, that's when you start to get old. So yeah, my friends thought it was a mental idea, but they probably thought, 'Well, obviously that's what Amin would do.' And they're right, it's what I would do to get what I always wanted.

BETH – SPAIN

There used to be this magazine that would go round every month and at the back you'd have other probation officers advertising their holiday homes to let. One month I spotted an advert for a place in La Manga, Spain, and just took a chance on it. Admittedly it was the cheapest one going, but I'd always wanted to own a holiday home in Spain myself, as had my Mum before me, and this break seemed like a great starting point. I loved it so much out there, that I ended up going practically every year for the next decade. The area is just absolutely beautiful. It's this spit of land, away from the mainland, that's surrounded by salt lakes. It's got beaches both sides, two seas to choose from, harbours, and great restaurants. Anyway, the plan was to initially have a holiday home there while I was working, and then retire out there later.

The Probation Service ended up being split in two and part

privatized in 2015, though. The public side continued managing high risk offenders, whereas the private side took the medium and lower risk. You were just automatically allocated to a side and I was allocated to the private side. For the first nine months it was great, but then we were bought out by another company and it became unsafe. The new company really didn't understand how dynamics change with people, depending on the circumstances in their life, so it often felt really volatile there. As a middle manager at the time, I was desperately fighting to keep our ethics and values, while at the same time supporting my staff. We were all on our hands and knees, just absolutely flooded with unstable cases, and it ended up really impacting on my health. So much so, that I was diagnosed with fibromyalgia. It's effectively a chronic pain and fatigue issue, and there's no cure for it. You can manage it, but who wants to manage something like that? I was really ill, I was off work a lot, and I ended up taking voluntary redundancy. That broke my fifteen years of continuous service, so all my benefits and my health care were impacted. It just all hit me hard, it really did.

Once the kids had left home, once I'd broken that continuous service, and once my health was impacted, the idea of living in Spain for at least part of the year was appealing. I'd always need to come back and take a three-month contract or so for the money, but it still gave me enough time to relax and enjoy life again. So, I downsized into an apartment and started looking for properties out there. While doing that, I met my fiancé, or my ex-fiancé as he is now. He'd previously lived and worked in Spain before as an estate agent and he really wanted to go back. In fact, he really pushed me into the idea. So, the plans were set, we found a place, and we headed out there.

Two months into living in Spain, finally fulfilling this dream, I found a lump again. It's sod's law, isn't it? I'd previously had skin cancer though, where they'd found a malignant melanoma and everything. I'd had an operation where they look lymph nodes out from under my arm, tested them, and then fortunately they told me it hadn't spread. This time, I found a lump in my breast. The thing is, I knew that nine out of ten of those were benign, and as I'd been through that experience previously, I just didn't think it was that bad. I just assumed I'd need treatment again, that it would all be fine, and I wasn't that worried about it. I booked a doctor's appointment for when I went back, and a biopsy, and then returned to Spain without any worries.

I'm very much a positive, forward thinking person. I'm able to push things to the back of my mind until I need to worry about it. I'd been back in Spain for a few days when I got the call to find out that it had spread to my lymph nodes. That was the first time I remember being devastated and in total shock about it. I was just looking at my partner and I was in total, utter shock. This doctor is talking about the process and the chemo, and I couldn't take any of it in. She was saying that I had to go back as soon as possible and that I needed six months treatment in the UK. An hour after that phone call, my partner received his own phone call, and he was offered a job in Spain. Everything was just put-on hold because of my news, though, so he had to turn down the job, and we had to come back to England.

I'd just accepted the fact it was happening at the time. I'm a very practical, logical person, and I felt I was able to put everything on hold for those six months. I'd go back, have the treatment, and then the dream could restart again. That's what I was thinking. If anything, it was just a detour to that dream for me, a temporary setback. Admittedly, it ended up being a horrible, horrible period for me. I had a really bad reaction to the chemo, it attacked my body so much that my immune system barely existed, and I nearly died at one stage. It's just like poison being pumped into your body, chemo. You can feel your whole body buzzing with it at times, too. It was a really awful time. I've never felt so rubbish in my whole life. I was just this shell of a person. I couldn't talk, I couldn't think, I couldn't form my thoughts. I just felt like I had no personality, that I was a different person. It was a really bad, bad time.

Initially, my partner seemed able to deal with it all and offer me support. As time went on though, he was getting increasingly angry and snappy and he really wasn't coping with it all. By the time the treatment had ended, and I arrived back in Spain, he'd totally changed. He was just awful to me. He was nasty, he was abusive, he was just awful. My natural instinct at the time was just to deal with it myself, that he was just suffering with stress, that we'll still work through it all. It just didn't change, though. We were due to get married that following year, we'd booked the wedding and paid for everything, but a few months after I arrived back in Spain it was all over.

We'd agreed that he'd support me for six months while I recovered out there, as we'd put all our money into the wedding and a business we'd opened, but then we had this big argument, and he wouldn't give me anything. He just walked out and literally left me with absolutely no money. It really was awful. My friends were having to lend me money to help me pay my bills and stuff. I suppose I felt sorry for myself at that stage. It was my whole life, my whole future, and that was all crashing down beneath me. I'd introduced him to this amazing place and then he just trampled all over my dreams for me.

I had a period of six months back in England and it did make me consider whether I could go back, knowing that he was still there and seeing other women. However, I thought to myself, no, I'm stronger than this, I'm going back out, I'm starting my own business, I'm not going to rely on anyone else.

It's a good job I'm stubborn, isn't it?

SWAPPING SCHOOLS

DAN – PERU

We're both teachers, me and my wife, and we both enjoy being teachers, but we were just fed up with doing that in the UK. You don't get paid enough for the work you're doing there, and that imbalance between your salary and your workload is draining after a while. And when we talked about it, neither of us were really living the life we wanted to live. So, we just started looking for more sustainable options. It's not that we were particularly looking at Peru at the time, but jobs came up that we liked the sound of, and we just went for it.

Peru sounds really exotic, doesn't it? And it certainly felt like that back then. It felt like an adventure to us. We were going to a city that we didn't really know and to a country we hadn't been to before. Our friends and family were a bit shocked when we told them. I don't think they saw the appeal or really understood why we were doing it. In fairness to them, when you're living in Watford, Peru probably isn't somewhere you consider moving, is it? The thing is, the job looked good, the school looked great, so what was there for us to lose?

We had a rather dramatic arrival in Peru, though. They picked us and another teacher up from the airport in a minibus with all our bags, and on the drive to the hotel, about fifteen minutes into the journey, someone smashed the window in on my wife and tried to steal her handbag. That was our 'What have we done?' moment, for sure. We sat there in shock, with glass all over us, wondering what we'd let ourselves in for. The hotel then always held that memory, and we had that reminder every day we returned there, too. Getting out of there and moving into our own apartment within two weeks helped, and we settled relatively quickly from there. Fortunately, and fingers crossed and touch wood, nothing has happened since to us. I do have colleagues that have been mugged at gun point, but no one has ever been hurt during that. There is that constant risk, though.

We live in Lima and it's a big, big city. It definitely feels bigger than London, too. The area we live, it's relatively wealthy with a lot of ex-pats, a lot of hotels, and a lot of tourists. It's not the wealthiest, but it's certainly up there. And then you have the shanty towns and slums, up in the mountains and in the areas surrounding the city. It's certainly not as bad as some of the wider districts in the country, but you do see homelessness. That's definitely still a problem here. A lot of the people, their livelihood is often standing at traffic lights and trying to sell cans of coke, chocolate bars, or they'll even do a little performance for tips while you're waiting for green. It's common here, and a constant reminder of the differences in lifestyles. It's interesting, though. There's a sense of community within Peru, and they'll help each other out where they can. You'll find that a lot of the taxi drivers will wind down their windows and buy something, so there's a constant market for these things.

With the school itself, we follow the British curriculum here, but it's not quite a British school. We have kids from three-years old, all the way up to eighteen-years old, and I teach maths in the secondary school part. The kids are all Peruvian kids, but they're the wealthy, well-to-do Peruvian kids. So, by the time they get to me, their English is near enough native for most of them. Most of us teach in English, but there are some subjects taught in Spanish, too. That's the real selling point for the school, that the kids come out speaking great English and can come straight out into the business world without any issues.

I think some of our friends and family think we're coming back any minute, but we've been here six years now and it's not really in our plans. When we do go back to visit, it's always interesting talking to friends that are still there. Their lives are very different to ours, but then their lives are probably what they imagined they were always going to be like. I can't say that mine is, though. Growing up, I don't think I once thought about living in Peru. We find that we don't have much in common with those friends now. There are exceptions, but in general this way of life has changed the way we see ourselves and what's important in life. I think this has broadened our horizons, for sure.

I'm not sure we'll stay here forever, though. We're thinking of heading to the other side of the world if we do move, probably Japan or Thailand or somewhere like that. We haven't got any firm plans though, and we're not in a rush to leave. Every now and then I browse jobs, look for anything interesting, but it's not something we'd do right now. As a maths teacher, I'm constantly told that I need to go and teach somewhere that actually appreciates maths, which neither the UK nor Peru really do. I often get the standard, 'Oh, maths, really?' responses from people whenever I tell them what I do.

ADAM – NIGERIA

The headteacher called me into his office with what he said was good news. I could apparently complete the rest of the year there, which was great, but that there'd be no job for me the following school year. Not the good news I was expecting, but that happens in teaching. I just went home, jumped online to look for jobs, and stumbled across a huge number of overseas roles. My eyes just lit up. I'd travelled as a student, enjoyed that at the time, and just thought, 'Hang on a second.' I started sending out applications to places across the world, a shit load of them in fact. I got some responses, had some interviews for places like Spain, and then ended up meeting another school owner in a hotel bar in London. Within a week, they'd offered me the job. They thought I'd be the perfect fit for them, which I hoped was a compliment, but I didn't really know. I just remember putting the phone down, walking in to see my brother, and casually going, 'Well, your brother is moving to Nigeria!' That shocked him. We did then have to get the atlas out and look up where Nigeria was, to be fair.

On the day I was due to fly out to Lagos, I was just sat in the living room physically shaking. I looked as white as a sheet, too. The realisation that I was going to Africa for the first time, let alone moving there, just hit me. I had no idea what to expect. I'd spent time in Central America before, so I knew what it was like to live abroad, but in Africa? No idea at all, mate. I ended up being one of only four Caucasians on the flight in the end, with the others being the staff moving out there with me. It was that moment when I realised how different it was going to be, how it was a whole new world.

Lagos is a city of over twenty million people, and it's an absolutely incredible barrage of sights, sounds, and smells. You see so much, and it can take six or seven hours to get across the city if you're stuck in traffic. Everyone lives on top of each other there, too. The thing is though, our school catered for the elite and the privileged, so for the first year I'd mainly see the nice parts of the city and I treated some of that time like a holiday. I wasn't paying for accommodation and we were staying in this compound for teachers, which was on this island in a new residential part of the city. I'd spend weekends on private piers, with the ex-pats welcoming us in and showing us their bars. We'd also have children of embassy staff at the school, so we'd get invited out to the embassies for drinks and the like, though we were never allowed to swim in their pools. I always thought that was a bit of a shame, myself. The school itself was nice, too. I'd be teaching classes of fifteen kids, mostly ex-pats or wealthy Nigerians who'd been abroad. I'd have a few Indians, a few Pakistanis, and some Brits in my classes, too.

One of the initial surprises, the owner of the school told us she'd hired a house boy for us, and he was coming around three times a week to clean and prepare our meals. Apparently, we could ask him to do anything for us, which was a little uncomfortable. We also had drivers and could hire them on the weekends. We were never allowed to invite these drivers into the house, they'd have to stay outside with the security guards. The school, bless them, did do a great job and really looked after us, but it wasn't really that local experience I wanted at times.

In my second year though, some of the local guys would gather and watch football and I'd go with them. So, we'd be in this derelict place, sitting on some benches, watching the games on Nigerian TV, while eating some local stew, and having a few beers. I got to know the owner of one place, so he'd look after me when I went down. A few of the local boys might get upset at a foreigner being there, so he'd just vouch for me. We'd have some good laughs there, too. In the end, I was only paying 30p for the same beer I was previously paying £5 for in the ex-pat bars. We'd also go to this bar; well, it was more an area of grass where someone had put a fridge, a few chairs, and a BBQ. You used to go and sit by the river, have a few beers, and have this barbecued meat or catfish and fries. It was absolutely beautiful, I loved that.

Nigeria has this reputation for email scams, and it sounds like an awful stereotype, but unfortunately fraud really is omnipresent there. There's this fraud code, the 419, the section of Nigerian law that deals with this type of thing. And there's songs about 419, there's references to it, you see buildings for sale, and they'll say, 'Not a 419', just in case. The thing is, Nigeria is the most populated country in Africa and it's a really expensive place to live. The oil money there has made an uber elite and everyone else is desperate to get their money. People are desperate, mate. They used to say, 'Be careful in December as it's robbing season', as they needed money to support their family at Christmas. It's a sad situation. There were always armed robberies going on. You'd see guns and violence quite frequently. You'd hear stories that a few of the children at our school, their families would suffer armed robberies. There was also a shoot-out when a bank near the school was attacked, so I definitely experienced the more violent side of the country, too.

I stayed there for two years. I knew I was moving on by the time that contract ended. I'd had malaria a few times and I was getting a bit tired of the mosquitos by then.

AMY – USA

We were living in Stockport back then, just outside of Manchester, with my parents coming from Yorkshire originally as high school sweethearts. My Dad was made redundant there and he was looking for jobs. This was in the late '80s, and from what I know, it wasn't easy for many people in the North then. He fortunately found two jobs, one was down in Plymouth and the other was in San Francisco, California. The Californian option was to work for two years in what became Silicon Valley, teaching people to use voice over IP, and that's ultimately where we went.

Would you rather live in Plymouth or San Francisco? It sounds an easy answer to most people, right? It was a more difficult decision than it appears on the surface, though. It meant leaving extended family behind and taking three small children to the other side of the world. In those days, there was no Skype, no WhatsApp, we just had very expensive phone calls, a fax machine, and long-distance letters. It really meant a lot to uproot and take the kids that far away from their grandparents, too. While it was difficult, my parents always had this spirit of adventure and this sense of, 'If not now, then when?' So, as a four-year-old, I moved to America with my parents, my older sister, who was seven at the time, and my younger sister, who was two.

It was a really different transition for each of us. My older sister went straight to Elementary School, where she ended up getting lunchtime detention for refusing to read out loud in class. She just didn't want the other kids to hear her English accent, and it's sad when I look back and think she got punished for that. With me, despite already going to school in England, I was too young for the American system and had to wait until the following year. While I was the same age as the kids when I restarted, they didn't really know what to do with me. My accent shifted to American fairly quickly, even if I did have kids coming up to me and asking if I could say something in English. By the time I went to middle school or high school, no one would know that I was English unless I told them.

My Mum kept a book of our experiences, and it's funny to look back and read all these stories now. At first, we were very much the English people who'd just arrived in the city. Yet on our first Thanksgiving, I was appalled as a five-year-old that we weren't doing the same as everyone else at school. They were all spending time with their family, they were having turkey for dinner, and we'd all made crafts for the holidays. Yet, we were going camping somewhere instead, taking advantage of the extra few days off work and school, and that was it. I had a strong desire at that age to be doing what my friends were doing and to really embrace being an American. It was a really big deal to me that we participated, that it was our life now, and we needed to do the same. My parents eventually relented and made some Turkey meatloaf in a camping trailer, somewhere in Northern California.

Growing up, whenever I didn't fit in with my American peers, I just pinned that on being English and different. So, when I got the chance, I spent a year studying back in Manchester. I was finishing off my degree, but I was also seeing what it would be like to live closer to where I was from. When I was there, I was working on a project about identify and figuring out how English or American I was. I thought there was a part of my identity missing when I was growing up, so I thought if I went to Manchester, I might be able to find it. As it turns out, that's not really how identity works. It's not like I just turned up, and everything instantly made sense, as it still didn't.

After moving to London once I'd graduated, I met loads of people who had these same cross-cultural experiences. Third Culture Kids is the term. It comes from a book by David C. Pollock and Ruth E. Van Reken called 'Third Culture Kids: Growing up Among Worlds', and it describes the experiences of globally mobile kids, moving because their parents are in the military, or are diplomats, missionaries, or international businesspeople. Often, they go to international school, they move every two to three years, and they'll have at least two languages under their belts. These kids, it turns out, create their own third culture out of their influences. It's an umbrella term, though, and you'll find loads of cross-cultural people identify with it, even if they aren't exactly a TCK on paper. I'm not one, I just went to the local school, I only speak English, and my family only did one big move, but I really identify with that book. The idea that you grow up between worlds, I can really relate to that.

To this day, I don't feel fully English, and I don't feel fully American, either.

JANE – SPAIN

My grandfather had a very bad heart attack when I was a kid, and back then they recommended that he lived in a much warmer climate to recover. My grandparents had always had a holiday home in this part of Spain, so it was decided that moving across here was best for him. At the time, my parents decided that it all sounded like a great adventure and they went for it, too. So, before you know it, I moved from Hertfordshire to Catalonia.

I remember my first day at school. I absolutely hated it. My mother was against us going to an international school, as she'd seen a child from another family not learning the language properly after going there. So, she decided to chuck us both in the deep end, me and my sister, and it worked to be fair to her. We went to an all-girls school, which was strange for me, having previously been to a mixed school. I just remember everyone crowding around me, talking to me in Spanish, and I understood absolutely nothing. It was very confusing. We were a novelty to them for a while. We were the only foreign children in the school and we just seemed to stick out. Me especially, as I'm blue eyed and have blonde hair, so I felt like I stood out for a long, long time. My sister was fourteen at the time, so she had it a little harder than I did, but it worked out for her in the end. We've both ended up fluent in both languages, and my sister went on to study her degree in Spanish, too. At that age, you're like a sponge and you just take everything in. Eventually, I really started to like it. Being at a private school, we were taught things like manners and how to lay a table. I doubt they do that now, but it felt relevant at the time.

I did initially have trouble with the school dinners, I'll admit. They were just so different. Half of the things, I didn't even know what they were. My sister and I were on different timetables in the dining room and they wouldn't let you out unless you'd finished everything. That first day, they gave me savoury rice and I'd never had that before. I was just sitting there, staring at the rice about an hour later until my sister arrived. 'It's just rice, Jane', she said. And I remember turning around and asking where the milk was, as I'd only ever had rice pudding at home before. It was just stupid things like that which can seem daunting to a kid, but you learn to be brave, to try new things, and then suddenly you've got this explosion of tastes. I rarely eat English food now.

We first moved to a coastal town, and then we moved slightly inland to a village, just a small Catalan village, and we've lived there ever since. It's funny as we came here because of my grandparents, but they couldn't settle and eventually moved back to England. We stayed, my parents opened a business, and I've always been happy here. Over time, I found that you can keep some of your British personality, but you do have to adapt, open your mind, and learn from the country you're living in. I think it's awful when people move and try to turn this into Britain. You tend to find these British communities, and other foreign communities in fairness, and they don't mix with anyone else and they don't adapt to the Spanish way of life. As a result, they don't have any Spanish friends. That's when you hear people saying that the Spanish aren't very friendly, they don't like us, and things like that. If you don't adapt to their country, then they're not going to like you, are they? What's the point of going to another country if you just want everything to still be British? I'm very proud to be British still, so long as I'm not mixing with the drunks who are falling about on the coast. I just wish people would open their minds, there's so much more that this country can give you.

I don't see myself living in England again, ever. I love to go back there, I love to visit, and I always cry when I leave, but I don't think I'll ever go back to the country permanently. I've never really lived there as an adult, though. I didn't have a say in leaving, but I do have a say in going back if I want. I don't really want to do that, though.

BEN – UKRAINE

I was working as a teacher in Nottingham, having done my teacher training there. After finishing my probationary year though, I resigned. It got to October half-term and I'd just had enough. I figured there had to be more to my life than sitting there teaching these horrible kids, and even though I didn't have a job to go into, I just quit. My initial idea was to either teach abroad in China, just doing English as a foreign language there, or take a break from teaching altogether and go traveling for a bit.

While thinking that through, I just posted on LinkedIn that I was looking for a job and sent my CV out to a few recruitment companies. The very next day, I had a call from one of them to ask me if I was interested in teaching geography at a private school in Kiev. Technically, I teach history, but I think there was a sheer desperation to get someone in and they didn't see the different subject as an issue. The interviews were all over Skype, and before long I'd signed up to a six-month contract to work in Ukraine. I was offered a two-year contract, but I wanted to take six-months in case I didn't like it. Almost like a trial. It ended up being a bit of a rush, I resigned in the October and was living here by the January. It meant that the nerves couldn't settle, and that was probably better for me. The longer it had taken, the more trepidation that would've built up, I think.

My family knew I was unhappy teaching in Nottingham, but there were some shocked faces when I said I was heading to Ukraine. They knew about the China idea, or that I might be traveling, but to be heading to what many see as a war zone?

That was a shock. To be fair to them though, I'd never thought about moving here myself. I'd never been, knew nothing about the country other than the football, and had signed up to work there. I just figured, if the worst came to the worst and I really hated it, I could just leave after a month.

I knew it was going to be cold and I'd been out to buy jumpers and the like, but that cold really hit me as I stepped off the plane. It was absolutely freezing. There was snow and ice on the ground, it was grey, it was bleak, and it all felt a bit melancholy. I wasn't there for long though. I went out there on a ninety-day tourist visa, dropped everything off in Kiev, and then left the country again. You need to leave the country in order to then return and collect your new working visa for Ukraine, so the school had booked me return flights to Georgia. So, I spent Orthodox Christmas in Tblisi, which was awesome. I was spending time in bars having drinks while everyone around me was celebrating their Christmas. It was a really cool experience, pretty unique, too.

Once back in Kiev, it did take a bit of guts to get out and see the city at first. There were times when I considered moving on, too, but stuck it out and I'm glad I did. That six-month contract quickly became a two-year contract, and I think the change in teaching environment has really made a difference. We've got much smaller class sizes, so instead of having sixty kids, I've got ten in my year. Stepping away from that teaching life in the UK, you can really see why people complain about it. My work life balance here, when I sit and think about it, is far better. Back home, I'd be marking books on a Saturday and planning lessons on a Sunday. Here, I still have work to do, but I can plan to the strengths of the children more and make sure they fully understand everything. If not, the parents will be onto me. The school caters for wealthy Ukrainians, so we have children from some high-profile families here. We've got security gates, guards with guns, and you'll also see these huge SUVs sat outside and they're often the personal security for the kids. So, the workload is different and there is pressure from the school and the parents, but it's nowhere near as bad as in the UK. I feel lucky, really.

In my day-to-day life, I wouldn't know the country was at war. Like my family, I was concerned at first and I did think about what would happen if the area was invaded, but fortunately there's been nothing unsettling. Obviously, you do have the issues in Donbass and Crimea, but that's all in the East and we don't have that daily contact. Some of my colleagues worked here during the Ukrainian Revolution and unfortunately one of our librarians had to emigrate from the Donbass area because of the conflict, but that's the closest I've come to it.

There are times when the reality of living in Ukraine hits me, especially when I look around at the Cyrillic language and understand very little of it. However, what's the alternative? Sit at home, live that small-town British life? Do you know what I mean? I think there's much more to life than that. The whole world is open to me if I decide to work on this international circuit, so I might see where I'm needed in future. I wouldn't go to anywhere like Syria, obviously, but I know I'd never go back to England and start teaching there again.

JANINE – SCOTT & RUSSIA

Janine: I moved here because of a sponsored Facebook post, of all things. It was by an English-speaking nursery and primary school, and they were asking for staff to come and work in the Moscow Oblast area in Russia. I've always been fascinated by this country and keen to visit, as had my family, so it really caught my eye. In fact, the first film my parents saw together was Dr Zhivago. Then, from there, my sister is named after the main character, Tonya, and then my eldest niece is named after the other character, Lara. So, it really does run in this family. Anyway, I saw the same post three years ago, responded back then, met the director in London for an interview, but then decided not to come over because of health reasons. Then last year, they emailed me and asked how my health was and whether I'd still be interested. Having taught for over twenty-five years, mainly in the Watford area, I thought it was finally time to try something new and give Russia a go.

I went over in half-term for a visit, taught there for a week, and the boss gave me a contract at the end of that week and asked me to think about it. I just took a pen and signed it, there and then. It was an easy decision for me. I'd absolutely loved that week and was confident it would work for me. They then asked me if I knew of any teaching assistants who'd like a job, and conveniently I did. I've known Scott for over ten years, and he'd been my teaching assistant when I previously worked with an autistic child. They made me get my phone out, ring him up on the spot, and ask if he wanted a job in Russia.

Scott: I was devastated when she first went, to be honest. I knew it was her adventure and I was happy for her, but I knew I was going to miss her. I always just thought I'd come and visit for time to time, and then she phones offering me a job. My first thought was, 'Yes, get me out there.' I'd only ever heard positive comments and had a friend out in St Petersburg, so I wanted to get out there and see it for myself.

Janine: My sister's initial reaction was, 'Did you say Russia? Why would you go to Russia?' In fact, quite a few people wondered why we were doing this. They kept saying we could go to sunny Spain, could go to Ibiza, could go to Marbella. The more they've heard though, the more they're coming round to the idea. I call it an adventure to them, as it really has been. People have started asking if they can come over, too.

Swapping Schools

Scott: Sometimes the stigmas stay from whatever terrible thing happened years ago, like the war and the football. It really sticks. People can't open their minds to the idea that a place like Russia could change. In reality, it's been great, hasn't it? I think the story of our first night in the country, that's definitely something to share. We went to this bar, and there's a live UFC match being shown. It was a big deal as this famous Russian fighter, Khabib, was fighting that night. It was great fun, but the night just got better and better for us. The owner of the bar comes over, this famous commentator joins us, and we're suddenly taken into the VIP room. We were meeting all these famous singers and actors; it really was a crazy night. We'd just arrived, too, and we didn't know anyone at all.

Janine: That commentator, he works on lots of Russian sports channels and a year later, he's still a friend of ours. He translates and speaks in English. So, yeah, on our first night out, we'd already met some pretty cool people. We also got invited to an arm-wrestling championship, and after that we were taken into a private room and we were fed this whole big spread, given lots of vodka, and were surrounded by world champion arm wrestlers. We met this sixty-year-old world champion and his agent, and there's us just looking small in comparison. It was bizarre. In general, there's this nonsense about Russians being stone faced and cold, but I've found the complete opposite. It's completely different to all the propaganda about the country, too.

Scott: Once you get to know them, they're a friend for life. Absolutely. Apparently, back in the day, you just didn't share who your friends were openly, or you didn't smile at people in case the police were suspicious of them. They'd then connect you to that person, which isn't good. It might well be a myth, but we've read it a few times. Early on here, we got on a bus and we had no idea what to do. This stony-faced old babushka

111

made some noises, we got the idea and carried on, and then she pointed out where our stop was. We wouldn't have known otherwise. So, she was still stony-faced, but still very helpful.

They love that we're English here, they want to talk to us and ask questions. Then once you've made friends, they really want to look after you. I'm constantly asked by locals for what I like about the country and they always want to know more.

Janine: You'll get people who hear that you're English, ask you where you're from, want to listen to you speak. Sometimes you'll feel like a celebrity, as a result. So, yeah, there's very little I dislike here. I'm accident-prone Annie, though. The very first snow and ice that we had, I was walking back to our flat and both my feet went from underneath me. I basically landed on my head. I managed to grab my phone and begged Scott to come and find me.

Scott: I ran out and found her halfway up the road.

Janine: We were taken in an ambulance and a translator from the school was sent. She was amazing. The doctor treated us like we were very special.

BEN - GERMANY

Just a few weeks before my fifth birthday, we packed up and moved to Saarland, close to the French border. My parents had always wanted to live abroad, and with my Dad working in the automotive industry, Germany seemed like the natural choice for it. I was too young to really know what was happening, but I think they saw it as an adventure and an experience for everyone. I do know that I spent that birthday sat on my own, with no friends, feeling pretty sorry for myself, though. Not quite the experience I was looking for, as you can imagine.

I knew no German before moving there, in fact none of the family did. While my parents had to take language lessons, the rest of us were just sent off to the local school. I went straight into Kindergarten, so was able to learn the language naturally. I was the perfect age for it all and just slipped into life there quite happily, apart from that first birthday. I wore cycling shorts, I had a big square, space theme backpack that I absolutely loved, and I got a cone full of stationery and treats on my first day at school. For me, that was my culture, that was my natural language, and that was the life I was living. If anything, I'd have probably classed myself as German at the time. It helped that I hadn't established a life for myself back in the UK, really. For my older brother though, it was really tough. He was at that awkward age - about six or seven - and the idea of going to the local school absolutely terrified him. There were no English lessons, in fact there was no spoken English at all, so he really struggled. I vividly remember being with my mum and dropping him off at school first and just watching him cry, as he just really didn't want to be left alone there.

Looking back, I didn't have a British identity at the time. I was born in Britain, to British parents, and I held a British passport. It's just no one at school knew anything about that. It was never discussed, no one ever asked me about it. I just fitted in there, I had the accent, I was accepted. That changed when I was eleven though, as we moved back to the UK. I then had that same experience my brother had. It felt horrible. I was settled in Germany, I had a big group of friends there, and I really didn't want to move back.

You know how people talk about being sad, alone, and struggling to fit in when moving to new places? I had that in reverse. For me, moving back to the UK was sad. And I'll tell you what, the kids in this country were absolutely horrible, too. I got picked on because I was different. I was bullied for bringing that

German culture over with me. There I was, in cycling shorts and carrying that big backpack, and the other children just really didn't take to me. I had no idea that I needed a new backpack, it just really didn't occur to me. If anything, I really didn't recover from that until I went to university, either.

Despite living abroad as a kid - and the idea wouldn't scare me now - I just don't have that wanderlust that some people seem to have. A lot of people who bounce around and live in different places, they seem to be seeking happiness in a place. It doesn't work for me like that. Having moved around a lot, and having been uprooted many times, I have learnt that I find happiness with who I am and who I am with, not where I am.

HELEN - UNITED ARAB EMIRATES

As a teacher, you get emails throughout the year asking if you'd consider working internationally, and as teachers are treated poorly back home, we eventually took advantage of that. Unfortunately for me, I can't teach English out here as I needed to have studied it at university, so it's the first time since I was 16 that I've been without a job. Fortunately for us, my husband studied English back in Nottingham, and he was the one head hunted for a role out here. So, we both left our jobs, and came out to the Emirates on his contract. His work was great to us. They booked our flights, put us in a hotel for a week, and then gave us the keys to our rent-free apartment from there. They also took us to IKEA and a few other places to get us settled, so that was a really different experience for us.

Everyone seems to know Dubai, but no-one really knows Abu-Dhabi. And if I'm totally honest, I didn't know much about it before we arrived. We got here at half seven at night and it was about 37 degrees, so the humidity just hit me. My fingers and toes swelled up and I remember just really hoping that this wasn't year-round. Fortunately, between October and April it does cool down, but we're still talking 20 degrees on the average day. The fact that the sun is out though, that's a massive contrast to being in the UK. It just really changes your mood to see that every day and gives you such a brighter perspective on things. What also helps is the slower pace of life out here. Once you get used to that pace, it can really improve your quality of life. The lifestyle itself is great and when you go out, it can feel like you're on holiday. In fact, we've been here for years now and I still feel like that a lot of the time.

Being Black is interesting here. I'm Black British with Ghanaian heritage. My parents emigrated to London around the same age as I am now. Growing up in the UK, I was the only Black girl in my class. It often meant I ended up being treated like the spokesperson for anything Black. I was constantly asked for hip-hop lyrics, people always assumed I was a natural dancer, just little things like that. I always felt like I was representing the whole of the Black race, and that really adds a lot of pressure. People were often just curious, in fairness, but then you have the times when you're followed in a shop, or you're perceived as being the angry Black girl if you're just standing up for yourself. Yet when we moved here, it was very different. It's really like being on the other side of privilege here. It's no longer about my race, but now about my passport, the way I speak, the way I live. Because I'm considered Western, rather than just Black, I'm treated far more favourably because of it. It's still not ideal, though, don't get me wrong. But it works out better for me because it's just no longer about my race but my nationality.

In the Emirates, 90% of the population are foreigners. Only 10% of people are local to the UAE. Emiratis are very proud of where they come from and 'looking after their own' is embedded in their identity. The government look after their own people and Emiratis are highly respected across the country. The way the government have created jobs for so many and those who have migrated tend to have a better quality of life compared to back home. But because we are from all corners of the world, this 'better standard of living' is always relative.

As a Westerner, and a British one at that, we live good. The remuneration packages to entice us into moving here have to be good, really. That's because we are used to a good standard of living back home and our governments have good relations, so they recognized that they had to give us added benefits. But this isn't true for all expats. We have expats from America, South Africa, Uganda, Kenya, India, Pakistan, Bangladesh, The Philippines, New Zealand, Australia, Colombia, you name it. Our experiences will vary vastly based on our nationalities. It also means that you can typically guess what a person does for a living here based on their nationality. Westerners are typically teachers or hold a professional position, people from the Philippines typically work in the malls, restaurants, or as nannies, Ghanaians and Nigerians are normally taxi drivers or they work in hotels and so on and so forth. There are, of course, exceptions to the rule. Irrespective of where we come from though, I'm sure most people would agree that the life they are living here is better than the life they lived back home. For me, that means I am afforded a privileged life of a British expat in the UAE whereas in the UK, I'm regarded as the daughter of immigrants. It's interesting to say the least.

TAKING CHANCES

BECKY – ROMANIA

I was very quiet about moving to Romania, if I'm honest. I moved in September, and I think I told my family in August. I didn't want them to put that seed of doubt in my mind. I had the job, I found somewhere to live, my flight was booked, and then I told them. The thing is, my family think the UK is a great place to be, that it's the greatest country in the world even. For me though, that concept of the greatest country just doesn't exist, and if it does then it's certainly not the United Kingdom. So, when I got the chance to move to Eastern Europe, to really see what living somewhere else was like, I took it.

The office manager at my company in Bucharest got the keys to my apartment the day before I was due to move in. So, I hadn't seen it with my own eyes before. It was on the ground floor of the block, it was dark and damp, and it had a cockroach problem. To top it off, there was a gas leak there in my first week. The landlord arranged for someone to fix it the following day and told me to sleep with the window open. I felt like I'd walked into those Eastern European stereotypes you often hear,

I really did. I didn't tell my parents though, telling them would give them that chance to go, 'We told you so.' While it was a miserable place, I just had this determination to make it work for me. I wasn't going to run back home because of some damp and some cockroaches, that would've made me feel like a huge failure and dump me back at square one again. I did, though, immediately start looking for a new place.

The apartment block I live in now, it was built in the '70s, so it's an old communist building. Until the pandemic happened, you had to pay your utilities in cash at a little kiosk on the ground floor, just like in communist times. The walls in my apartment are so thin, I can hear all my neighbours around me. I can hear them talking, I can even hear them sneezing, I can listen to what they're watching on TV. Having studied history and being fascinated by Eastern European history, I realized that maybe this wasn't a design flaw. It's very possible that it was designed like this to stop dissent against the regime, to give people the opportunity to monitor each other. Obviously, it's not like that today, but it does give me this sense that I'm living in history rather than just sitting at home reading about it.

Bucharest is a city that's still recovering from communism and you can really see that in the way people act. They don't form queues; they just push to get what they need. My colleagues explained that it's because they had to behave this way previously, that it's ingrained into them to hustle for something. You'll also find that where we'd put a jumper on if we're cold, and then add more layers if we're still cold, the Romanians will just turn up the heating. They tell me it's because they didn't have these luxuries during communism, so they're just enjoying it now. You can't really begrudge them that, can you? It's still one of the poorest countries in Europe and it's very corrupt in both government and day to day life, so you can definitely understand their mindset.

While there are Romanians who are critical of their

own government, and some people here are still struggling, they've always been incredibly welcoming to me. I'll strike up conversations with taxi drivers or people in supermarkets and they're always curious as to why I'm in their country and keen to hear what I like about it. It's a far cry from the way we treat Romanians who come to the UK, isn't it? We just tend to hear so much bullshit about them, that they're coming to take jobs or claim benefits. They're just economic migrants though, just like I am. I'm an economic migrant or immigrant, here to work and make a life for myself. Yet turn that around in the UK and there's a real stigma attached to the idea. People view immigrants negatively, and that sentiment has fuelled the way the country is governed.

I used to volunteer with refugees and asylum seekers as an English teacher in my local community back in the North. It really affected me. I heard their stories; saw the prejudice they face. I remember one instance where we finished class, in the city centre, and we walked out into an anti-immigration rally. It was difficult to walk through that and explain to my students what was happening. I think I lost a lot of hope in the UK then, in politics, and in society. I was really feeling like I needed to find that escape. I think Romania has been that escape for me.

Living in a new, big city, far away, where nobody knows me, where I can just be myself, it's been liberating and a really transformative experience. I still care about people, but I don't have the right to vote here, so I feel a detachment, that I don't have the same sense of responsibility here. It's by no means a traditionally beautiful city, but I still think there's a real beauty to it and in its people. I'm really glad I've done this.

HADEN – SLOVAKIA & CZECH REPUBLIC

I was a surfer, and my first job was in Bodmin, Cornwall. I suppose you could say I'm an ex-surfer now, though. I was surfing for many, many years. I had the typical long blonde hair, all of that. But when I was nineteen, my parents decided to emigrate. I guess they wanted a better work life balance and a new adventure. They tried for Australia, but couldn't get the visa points, and then tried for New Zealand and ended up moving there. I came home one day to find that I had six months to decide, either go with them or stay back in Cornwall. The thing is mate, I was happy where I was and thought I'd stay. Sounds mad when you think I could've surfed out there, doesn't it?

Anyway, I stayed, picked up a job at a big supermarket brand, and one day a guy there said he was off to another store in London and asked if I wanted to go with him. After a long weekend up there, I walked into this supermarket branch, spoke to the trading manager, and they offered me a job as a shelf-stacker. I figured it was a good time to get a career and make something of myself. I couldn't stay surfing in Cornwall forever, it's awful for careers in general and it's absolutely dead in the winter. And perhaps moving closer to London to get a job as a shelf-stacker would surprise people, but I had a plan. I picked a store with one of the worst turnovers of staff, as I thought I had more of a chance of progressing through the ranks there. I transferred the following week with my rucksack of clothes, rented a room from this granny who worked on the checkouts, and that was it.

I got my head down, got promoted, and eventually spent seven years as a trading manager. I was then looking after refits when a supermarket expanded and became a hypermarket, as it were. This was taking me around the London area, so I'd do stores in that region. It wasn't until I got the magic email that said, 'Would you like to go to Prague, all expenses paid, for three months?' that I'd even considered making a change. The idea was that I'd go out there as a consultant and help the local team with their takeover of another brand. Then they'd effectively be paying for my beer while I stayed in a nice hotel. Sounds alright that, doesn't it? I was single at the time and just thought, 'Why not?'

Unfortunately, I did one of those typical British things and, as it was the first time abroad, I left my passport on the plane. I got to immigration, tapped my pocket, realised, and thought I was going to die. I called the police officer over, explained it, and he told me I had to get back on the next plane and go back. I had to plead with him a bit, tell him I was there for work and needed help. They took me over to this typically Eastern European window, the type where you tap on it and someone looks through the shutters, leaves you waiting, and then eventually opens the door. He said I had to go back, too. I suddenly realised I had my driver's license on me, got that out, and he eventually let me through with the promise that I'd go to the British Embassy in the morning. I was then escorted through passport control with a police officer either side of me. I looked like a drug lord, effectively. Whereas really, I'd just fucked up. Then as soon as I tried checking into the hotel in Prague, the first thing they asked me for was my passport. Anyway, the receptionist I spoke to at the hotel, this Slovakian woman, she's now my wife.

After dating for a while, I had to go back to the UK to finish my project there. Fortunately, she agreed to come back with me, but we always knew it was temporary. Why would I go back to the UK after living in Prague? My parents didn't live there anymore, my friends weren't really in London, I just had nothing holding me back. Eventually I got a transfer back out, got married within twelve months and then had two kids, and I've never really looked back. I also didn't really hold back, did I?

Prague is a great place and I loved living there, but I do

hate the reputation it has for stag dos. Fair enough, I did have my own stag party there, but we tried to find the pubs and stuff that weren't as touristy or full of obnoxious lads. It's a bit embarrassing at times, especially when you're living there. We thought we'd escape the crowds one night and go sightseeing, me and my wife, and so we went to the Charles Bridge in the middle of night. It was empty and beautiful, but in the background, I could just hear drunken English lads singing, 'I love you, baby.' Unfortunately, that's not a one-off either.

We lived in the Czech Republic for two years before moving across to Slovakia, largely because we wanted the children to grow up there. There isn't a huge difference in life here, but you'll notice that the Slovaks are far more laid back in comparison. It's a little like moving from London back to Cornwall. Everyone seems friendlier, everyone appears more open, and they're far more approachable. I tried to integrate myself as much as possible here. I think it's important to do the things that locals do, see their country from their eyes, and understand how they feel and live.

I'm never going back to the UK, though. I'd rather clean toilets than go back to the UK, really. It's mainly because of the work life balance. It's nice to go back for a short holiday, but no longer. I've just paid my council tax here for the year and it was about 130 euros. For the whole year. The house I'm living in now, it's effectively a liveable garden house with a bio-tank and a well for water. So, I don't pay those big utility fees. If I go back and pay for South West Water again, I'll probably have a heart attack.

LIAM - USA & GERMANY

It was never a dream or a goal to live abroad, it just happened. It started when I moved to London after university. I didn't have any great plans other than being in the big city, and I just moved there for the experience. I slept on a mate's sofa for a week, started applying for jobs, and got one in ad-sales. I fell into this job, kinda enjoyed it, kinda didn't enjoy it, but stuck it out there for about four years. I then moved to a new role at a fairly successful American company who were opening an office in London but wanted experienced British staff to help them. They hired me as a manager, and I managed a team for them. They then purchased a German company, bought them out, and they had two offices in Berlin and Hamburg. Within nine months of me starting in London, they asked me to move to Berlin for a few months and help that office out, and it just went from there.

I was in Berlin for December and January, which isn't the greatest time to be in that city. It was just to babysit the office before they closed it down, really. It was right by Checkpoint Charlie, in this terrible, old fashioned, Eastern bloc style building. It was miserable. I did two months there and didn't particularly enjoy it. I was then asked to work in Hamburg and head up their office for six months. I had a very long-term girlfriend at the time and I always planned to go back to London, but after being there for two-months, they asked me to stay there permanently. At first it was tough. My girlfriend left me fairly early on, though it wasn't this big dramatic thing. She flew out, had the conversation with me in person, and then flew back. I'll always respect her for that. Moving abroad wasn't the reason for us breaking us, but it focused us on the problems we had in our relationship that we were probably ignoring. Having that distance gives you some perspective. She was the one brave enough to say something about it and I've always respected her for that. I think we both knew it was coming, though.

It was a whirlwind, initially. I was living in a different country, on my own, and work was incredibly difficult at the time. We were trying to turn this German company around, but we were getting hammered in the press and it was tough.

You have these first six months when it's quite exciting to be living abroad, and then the normality kicks in a bit. For me, that honeymoon period ended, my relationship ended, and work started getting tough. And all three things happened at the same time, so it was a real whirlwind. For that first year or two, it just wasn't fun. The reason I stuck with it was, was that it was a good professional opportunity. It's interesting when you're not really enjoying somewhere, but you have to stick it out for the professional opportunity. I'm sure a few people can relate to that.

After that first year, things changed a little. My experience of moving around so much, is that it takes about a year to build up a social community and a friendship group. You get to know the city. You start building up a group of people who you're excited to see, too. I was dating again and that's an interesting way to feel connected to a new place. Meeting people adds an enjoyable element, for sure. I loved it eventually, I had a wonderful time. I also joined a local cricket team in Hamburg and that gave me a real sense of purpose outside of work. The standard is as bad as it gets, but it was fun. I played in the German Bundesliga for cricket, which is a source of pride for me. I reached the pinnacle of cricket in Germany. It was a real mix of nationalities, though. Kiwis, Asians, Brits. We also had a social, charitable element, so we spent a lot of time with Afghanis and local teenage boys from those types of nations. It was great. It was a social thing, it was some competition, and gave a sense of purpose to the weekends. That helped me feel really settled, as well. However, I never, for one second, thought that I'd live in Germany for my whole life. It's hard to put my finger on why. I don't know why, I never felt drawn to it. I also started dating my wife fairly quickly, which no doubt had an impact.

I was only single for about six months. We met on a work trip to San Francisco, but she's from Texas and living in New York, and it just so happened that I'd already booked a personal, solo trip to New York for fun later that year. We ended up hanging out, having a good time together, and we both knew immediately that this was it. We both just said, 'We're going to get married, aren't we?' It was weird as I was with my previous girlfriend for six years and we hadn't even talked about moving in together, yet here I am talking about marrying someone. By that stage, I knew I wanted to be with her. It was just logistically never going to be Germany, that was completely off the cards. It was either going to the US or maybe even the UK. We did the long-distance thing, we'd maybe see each other once every six weeks, and we'd fly back and forth. Whilst still living on different continents, I proposed. I then spoke to work about it and they arranged for us both to move to the Phoenix office. They sorted me out with a visa, which was a game changer as that's normally very difficult, and then we ended up in Arizona together.

KERRY – SWITZERLAND & NICARAGUA

Before moving to Switzerland, I'd spent a while living and working in different parts of Latin America. It was kind of a gap year or eighteen months after university, and largely because I had these itchy feet and a real desire to travel at the time. I went with a friend and our initial idea was to work our way down from Central America and then into Argentina. We ended up staying for six months in Nicaragua, where we taught in a school during the day, then worked in a bar at night for the money. Looking back, I have a lot of respect for how calm my parents seemed to be about that whole idea. It was before regular internet and cheaper mobile phones, so we'd just go to an internet café once a week to catch up with people. This was before any political upheaval in the country and I never felt in any danger there, if I'm honest. I'm not sure if we were just being naïve at the time or completely oblivious, though. From Nicaragua, we made our way down to Panama, into Colombia, and then onto Ecuador, Peru, and finally onto Argentina.

Between Panama and Colombia, we were a bit stupid. We were full of these romantic ideas about travel and our first idea was to hitch a ride on an exotic yacht. We talked to several people but that never worked out. Then we came up with what, in hindsight, was a really bad plan. We went across to the San Blas Islands, got talking to a guy, and he hooked us up with some other guys who were sailing around the Darien Gap. We got as far as getting on this boat early one morning, having been to the police station the night before to register with them, before being stopped by those same police and warned that it wasn't a safe territory for tourists. At the time, we were gutted, and it felt like we were missing out on this big adventure, but we soon realised how stupid we'd been. It was a pretty sketchy boat, and it was planning to transport goods from island to island, so it really wasn't safe for us. That's an embarrassing story, I know, but it really showed us how young and inexperienced we were back then.

That time in Latin America, it ended up being a really nice taster to living abroad full time. I got to meet new people, work with kids in different places, and gained experience at learning different languages. It was also the first time I'd really understood the different levels of privilege in life, as it had felt more abstract back home. I ended up coming back to the UK with a very idealistic mindset, too. I remember advocating for all these charities and watching my family just roll their eyes at me, but I can completely understand now I look back at it. I'd have no desire to do that travelling again today, but at the time it was all I was thinking of. I couldn't get my head around the idea that people didn't want to do it.

Once back home, I did my masters, graduated, and then went to do a PhD in Scotland. It was there that I started studying parasitology, which allowed me to work with people from all over the world. Working in scientific research, it's really an international experience at times. I ended up with friends from very diverse backgrounds, very different personalities, and from completely different cultures. So, when the opportunity to do a post-doctorate opened in Bern, Switzerland, I just jumped at the chance.

My boyfriend and I broke up about six weeks before I left for Switzerland, and at first it was difficult and exhausting to settle down here. I was disappointed about the relationship, a bit out of my depth, and there were a few times in the first year that it felt hard. It never crossed my mind to throw it in. I always had the impression that, even if it's hard work now, I knew it would get better. And it did. That initial contract was only for a year, but things just ended up working out in my favour and I'm still here ten years later with a son who is quickly becoming much better at Swiss German than me.

Bern is a great place to live, especially with the nature and having the river running through the city. That river has always been a big part of my summer here, really. I can go for a swim at lunchtime, or we can take a rubber dinghy up to the next town and float the 30km back with a beer, or we can have a BBQ on the beach. That's very special. We have the mountains here, too. That's something I don't use enough though; I've not really skied enough, and I've barely been hiking as much as I should. I'm always mad at myself for that, but nevertheless we've had some great times in the mountains nearby.

ED & KATH – SAUDI ARABIA & UNITED ARAB EMIRATES

Ed: I've spent most of my life abroad – I spent thirty years working in the gulf area, so Saudi Arabia, United Arab Emirates, Bahrain, and now I'm in Thailand. Before that, I was working in England as an electrical engineer, just outside of Liverpool. I got a phone call one day asking if I was interested in a job in Saudi Arabia, so I said, 'Hey, talk to me about it.' So, the guy phoned me and talked to me all about this job at Jeddah Airport, and then offered me a proper, technical interview. Got off the phone, told my wife, and she said, 'Oh, I applied for that job for you.' To cut a long story short, I got the job and went out to work at Jeddah Airport. Three months later, I got a phone call from a neighbour that goes, 'Do you know your wife is having an affair with my husband?' What a set-up, hey? So, that's how I started my career in Saudi Arabia.

I found it hard initially because I couldn't spend time with the children. We were having a little bit of trouble, which was one of the reasons I was going away, and I was working stupid hours to try and get money to keep everything going. The first six months there, we were working fourteen, fifteen hours a day. One company had taken over the whole airport, from thirty-nine other companies that previously ran it, so we were working tremendously hard to try and get it all up and running for them. Suddenly though, we went down to eight hours a day and five days a week, and I just found it extremely boring. So, I got into the tennis leagues, the squash leagues, sailing, camping, and everything turned out to be absolutely fantastic. I hardly had time to go to work! I went back to the UK after that, we talked, got divorced, and that was that.

After that, I spent twenty-five years in Saudi Arabia, first in Jeddah Airport, then in Riyadh for an American company who worked with the Saudi Air Force. That role was interesting, as they had numerous underground nuclear facilities and I'd teach people how you'd stay there for three months without any outside contact. I then met my new wife, Kath, a British nurse working in the country, and we married in Riyadh. How did you find it, Kath?

Kath: Working in Saudi Arabia as a nurse, that was quite an experience. The majority of my patients were Saudi, and they'd get admitted to the free hospitals where I worked. As the ex-pats there had to have private medical insurance, they'd often be at the private hospitals, and they'd only be admitted to a free hospital if they'd been picked up from a road accident. Anyway, back in 1983 when I first went out, the Saudi doctors didn't know the difference between the Western nurses and the local ones. Western nurses, like I was, are effectively autonomous practitioners. Yes, the doctors gave orders, and we'd follow them, but you didn't have to tell us absolutely everything. The doctors were often taken back by how assertive we were, but once they understood, they respected it.

One of the hospitals I worked at was very Islamic, and I was working as a supervisor there, which included the medical ICU and the dialysis ward. I remember there being a cardiac arrest, and I just hurtled down the corridor from one end to the other to put the patient on a ventilator. A few moments in, the doctor stops me and asked where my veil was. We had to cover our heads up, you see, but as I'd scooted down the corridor it must've been lost somewhere. So, I had to step away from this emergency and cover myself up. I couldn't believe it.

Being a woman, I'd often have some of the older, more traditional men request to have male nurses. We did that if we could, but it wasn't always possible. You'd also then get husbands who wouldn't allow their wives to be treated by male doctors. So sometimes, particularly in a delivery room, the husbands would just flat out refuse it. You've got a woman in the advanced stages of labour, and they'd have to take her away and wait. Sometimes you'll have a woman having a difficult birth, and she's left to wait as the husband doesn't want the male doctor there, so it could be dangerous.

Ed: And don't forget the time I had to give permission for your operation, of course.

Kath: Ah yes, that really pissed me off, that did. For the longest time, the issue of the male of the family directing operations really bothered me. We couldn't force something on the patient unless they're sectioned, but the females would often defer to a male and ask the nurses and doctors to talk to them instead. It shouldn't be this way in my mind, but you do need to be broadminded out there at times, that's for sure.

Ed: I always knew about the poor treatment of women in Saudi Arabia, but one of the things about working in a big company is that you were always isolated from it. The ladies weren't treated as well as the men, but they were able to do things if we didn't shove it up the noses of the locals. And I've learned that over the years. Looking back, I think I've had better opportunities, doing what I've done. Spending thirty odd years working abroad has been a great experience, and if I didn't like it, I wouldn't still be out here today.

HANNAH – KUWAIT

I had to google Kuwait when I was first offered this opportunity, I'll be honest. I was working as a personal stylist down in Brighton, but it was that classic retail job where they say you're being promoted to a personal stylist, but you're still on minimum wage. So, I was feeling really disenchanted. I'd been down in Brighton for a few years by this point and it wasn't really going the way I wanted. Then a woman came into the store one day, chatting away to me about being a personal stylist, and just asked me if I'd ever considered working for a luxury brand in Kuwait. I didn't know where it was at the time, but I did know the brand they were talking about. The conversation went from there, really. I was offered this sales position for the brand in Kuwait and I just felt like I had absolutely nothing to lose. I thought I could just go for a year, take this fantastic opportunity, and see where it went from there.

I'm really chatty, so I told everyone the minute I found out. I didn't know anything about the country, so I used it as a good chance to gather some reactions. On the whole, it was pretty negative. A friend of a friend had a horrible experience where she'd moved to Saudi Arabia and it had gone awfully for her, so that was at the back of my mind a little. The thing is the only person whose opinion I really valued, enough to change my own mind, was my Dad. I pitched it to him as, 'If you were me, would you go?', and he said yes. As soon as I heard that, I knew it was a good idea. I had always wanted to try living abroad and getting that experience, and sure, I wouldn't have initially picked Kuwait, but it didn't have to be forever.

I've never gotten on a one-way ticket flight before, and I think I just went into an immediate state of shock. I just got on with it for ages. The first three months of being here, I was like a little robot just tootling about, not really taking it all in as I went. I was just so overwhelmed with it all. I lost so much weight when I first moved here, too. I know this sounds ridiculous, but I just didn't know the food brands and I was a little scared of it all. I was just in shock for so long, but fortunately there were quite a few Brits who moved over for the same company and there was a proper crew of us. Before long, we were settled, and it ended up being one of the funniest years of my life. I sometimes think I could write a sitcom based on it; it was that funny. We arrived, realized the job was a bit shit and we were being treated like children, so we just reverted to acting like them. I've never laughed so much in my life.

Life here is drastically different to living in the UK. There's a more laid-back culture here. I always find it shocking when I'm back in London to see people commuting, as that just doesn't happen here. I get a taxi to work every day, it takes fifteen minutes. It's a very sedentary lifestyle in Kuwait and it's very easy to fall into doing absolutely nothing. As there aren't the bars and pubs here, the social scene revolves around going out for food and drinking coffee. Eating out or getting food delivered, that's just the norm. We don't cook at all, which sounds disgraceful, doesn't it? The issue is that importing food is generally quite expensive here, so if I went to the supermarket and bought the same items, then it'll probably cost me more than just ordering it. So, you get into this routine of thinking, 'What's the point?'

The most difficult thing about living here, is being exposed to very, very poor workers. There's also a lot of human trafficking issues, which is difficult to see and I find it very hard to witness at times. It's really opened my eyes to a lot of the injustices in this world. In the UK, we don't often see it at this level. When we're talking about migrant workers, it's often a concept and not a reality for most people. When faced with that reality here, it's heart-breaking. It's a real wake up call to some of the issues in the world. Any service person here is going to be a migrant worker. So, the guy who fills up your car, the lady in the supermarket, the taxi driver, the beautician, anyone you consider to be working in a service job, they're all poorly paid migrant workers. Even though it's awful to witness some of the poverty that I've seen here, I'm very grateful to have been able to see it. It's made me much more aware of the situation and of the injustices of this world. It's made me realise that I'm very fortunate to be British and see that we're effectively born with golden tickets. Sometimes we need to take a step back and realise how bloody lucky we are.

Looking at Kuwait on paper, you'd probably think, 'Oh my god, why would you ever want to live there?' However, I genuinely think it's a good place to live. Don't get me wrong, London on a nice day is still the best city in the world for me, but it's not like you live there and someone takes you by the hand and you go off and do these amazing things all the time. Wherever you live in the world, you need to make it work. You need to go out and do exciting things for yourself. I've been feeling for a while that I'm never going to be completely happy in any single place in the world. My life is so spread out, that I don't think it's possible to find the ideal place. I guess my attitude is that if I could adjust to life in Kuwait, then I can adjust to anywhere else. If you go in with that attitude, then you should be able to be happy anywhere.

LUKE – POLAND

I came to Poland at quite an interesting time, as I think I caught the back end of the old, traditional Poland. When I got to Bydgoszcz for example, the regional trains there were still pretty old. It was like sitting on a washing machine for three hours. They're shaking all over the place and they're jam packed with people. A lot of the restaurants, too, they'd only really offer Polish food back then. I think there was one Vietnamese place and maybe one Polish Mexican place in the whole city, which obviously wasn't as authentic as you'd want. Whenever you went to a restaurant in those days, you'd basically get cabbage with absolutely everything. Even a Mexican place, every single meal would come with cabbage. Back then, but I'm pretty sure it's changed, it used to be quite standard to see people sat around a table with a bottle of vodka on ice and just chasers to go with

133

it. It's what you'd imagine Poland was like, obviously. However, in the last few years, and especially now I'm in Poznan, you can really see the change. There's more variety, a lot more culture. You can really see that the middle classes have started to grow, that the EU funding has been well spent on infrastructure and the like. It's certainly an increasingly modern place, and a pretty good place to live, too.

It was chance that I ended up here, really. Throughout my twenties, I did a bunch of different jobs in the UK that I really didn't like. Office jobs, call centre jobs, quite a few sales jobs. Then, I was working for a company just outside Manchester and I was living on my overdraft every month. A month before Christmas, the company ran out of money, shut themselves down, and didn't pay us. I was kinda screwed. I moved back home and just thought, 'What the fuck am I going to do now?' My Dad was always on at me to become a teacher and I didn't want to go down that traditional route, so I thought I'd try English as a foreign language. After doing my teaching course, I was just applying for jobs all over Europe basically. Poland was the first place to offer me a job. I think I sent my application for that on the Monday. I had my interview on the Wednesday evening. Then I was offered the job on Thursday. Then I was in Poland, starting my job on the following Monday. It was a super quick turnaround. It was one of those things where I just thought, 'Great' and went for it. It was good though; I didn't have time to stop and think about it.

I haven't flown in ten years now after I started getting these claustrophobic panic attacks when I was onboard. So, my first journey across to Poland, was this twenty-four-hour coach that left Victoria coach station. I think I was the only English person on the bus, so it was a bizarre experience. I didn't speak any Polish at the time, and I was sat next to this big Polish guy, who was sat there just solidly drinking. He was jolly, talking away to me in Polish, and just getting more and more drunk as the journey went on. I also got introduced to the Polish lektor over movies during that journey. They put War Horse on the coach TVs, but rather than it being subtitled or dubbed, it was basically a guy speaking over the movie in Polish. It's not the commentary, but it's just one man that does all the voices. It's weird. I don't know if he's explaining something, but the effect as a foreigner is that you've got some guy talking over the English. You can just about hear it, but they seem to absolutely love that here. In Polish cinemas now though, all the movies are English with subtitles. The lektor is more old-school, it tends to be on TVs only now.

I arrived in the city, Bydgoszcz, at 7am in the morning and it was in December. The bus station was odd, the buses were really old, and it was all just these concrete blocks everywhere. The owner of the school came to collect me, and at first, he just didn't look anything like I was expecting. He ended up being a great guy, a really good boss, it just took me by surprise at first. He took me to the flat above the school and everything there was old. It was just a mish-match of old furniture. None of the flats there had proper beds at the time, either. They'd have a sofa that folds out into a bed, and that's the standard bed option here. It's pretty uncomfortable. That's changed now with things like Ikea coming in, but at the time it was pretty common.

I do really like living in Poland, I'll be honest. As an English teacher, most students appreciate having an English person to speak to. When you're out and about, people just want to speak to you when they hear that you're English. We'll be in a bar and people will invite us over, and in general be pretty welcoming. In terms of safety on the streets here, I feel way safer than I did in England. I worked in a bar in Manchester for a while, and you'd walk home through the city centre and you'd always see fights and trouble. Here, apart from one incident, I've never, ever seen a fight in a bar or in the streets. The guys, they aren't trying to impress women by being hard. I think they probably are really hard, but they don't feel the need to act on it.

FITTING IN

IAN – ITALY

I ended up being in Italy because I got made redundant. I was working in hotels and restaurants in London at the time, fairly top end stuff. I was sat there looking to get back into that, and my cycling club mate suggested that I should look into cycling coaching at the same time. You know what it's like while looking for work, you do need something else to focus on at times. I've always been a big fan of cycling and being out on my bike, especially at times when my wife was desperately trying to keep me in the house to do jobs, so much that I've probably spent forty odd years riding and racing. I've always been good with working with people, too, so credit to my mate, it sounded like a decent idea. So, I started building a website, did my British cycling exams, and in the end thought it would be a great career change for me. I was nearly fifty at the time but still thought it could work, so I wouldn't call it a midlife crisis at all. Having a supportive partner helped, though. She said we should give the idea a go for a year and see where it went.

So now, I'm sat near Lake Garda, working from home as

a cycling coach. Primarily, I spend most of my day in front of my laptop looking at statistics. I look at the data for people out riding, watching their heart rate and the like. And I'm working with global athletes here, not just those in the UK or Italy. Of course, I could've carried on doing that back in England, but my mother-in-law is Italian and the idea of moving across to Italy was always likely. Then you look at what we've got in this area, and you can obviously understand the decision. You have such a brilliant summer here, so for about six months of the year you just want to be outside. We have every sport here. Obviously cycling is the biggest one, as we have all the hills and the mountains. Then we've got the lake, so you've got sailing, boating, kayaking, and the like. You've then got abseiling, canyoning, skiing, running. You've got absolutely everything here. We've got big events like triathlon, too. It just made so much sense for us.

We were quite lucky when we did move across. The economy was doing well, it was pre-Brexit, and we had a good house in South East London that we could sell. That went quickly, and we used the money to buy a plot of land in Northern Italy. We had the house built from scratch, so waited two years to move into it, but they've done a phenomenal job. Foreign builders often have this dodgy reputation, and they do need chasing a little, but they've done a great job here. We also have this view of Italians being glamorous, but their modern building work does add weight to that. They want them to be bigger, better, newer, the latest. It all has to be like that for them, so that's why it takes a while for things to be built. The quality is fantastic though. We saw the architect's impressions and just a muddy field initially and it was hard to imagine, but it does look phenomenal now that it's finished. Even the plants they've used, they're great.

The building work might be newer, but I've noticed that Italians are often very worried about trying something new. Working from home, for example, it's all very new to them and a massive change. Italians don't really like taking a gamble on something. That applies to business, too. Everything is through word of mouth or recommendations, rather than looking online and risking meeting someone they've never worked with before. They could embrace technology more, that's for sure. They could take a risk, take a gamble, buy something online. I think that's the biggest thing that's holding this country back. It reminds me of someone stepping into a swimming pool when they don't like that cold water. They'll splash water on themselves, edge in, go back, say they don't really like it. That's a little bit like how Italians can be. They feel like they're stuck in 1990 at times.

When I first moved here, I knew a few words of Italian, but I learned early on that it was about embracing everything and throwing yourself into the life. You just have to go with it. Embrace it all, try it all, don't try to look for the English people only, embrace the way of life, just open your arms and take it. If you do, you'll enjoy it much more. You have to make friends, join communities, get involved. If you want to initially understand Italian culture, you should go to church here. You don't really have to be religious, but it's a massive part of life here and the churches are packed every weekend. The thing is, if you go to a church then you get to understand all the people that live locally. The Priest knows absolutely everybody, too. From where the best places to eat are, down to who's an arsehole and who isn't. It's a really good way to integrate into where you live, the people you live around, and for other people to get to know you. You avoid the gossip about you that way, too. You don't have to go for the rest of your life but starting off there for the first three months is a great idea. Just go, say hello to people, go and meet the priest and explain that you've just moved into the area. Religion won't be rammed down your throat there, trust me. It's a really big thing and it'll steamroller your journey into being embraced by the locals. You can feel alienated here if you don't go.

JANET – SWITZERLAND, USA, SINGAPORE, & HONG KONG

I stopped working in 2005 when we moved to Hong Kong. I was selling swimwear to stores back then, wholesale brands to retail stores. The problem was all my contacts in big stores, all the relationships I'd built up over the years, that just didn't translate into the Asian market. The labels said they didn't have the coverage out there, but I couldn't just go knocking on doors and telling them I had this great swimwear company. They might buy something, sure, but they'd prefer to work with people they know. That takes time to develop, and I didn't know how long I'd be living there, so I just stopped. I'd miss it at times, but I knew right from the start that this was going to take a mindset shift for me. I knew I had to get my mind around a different set of circumstances. Some people can cope with that, some people can't. The people that don't cope, it's often because they were always defined by their work and what they do. As a trailing spouse, regardless of whether you're the wife or husband, you've often been taken away from everything and it can really make you feel like you've lost your identity. Whether that's in Hong Kong, Singapore, the USA, or now in Switzerland, I've really worked hard on having the right mindset and keeping myself busy.

Hong Kong was one of the easiest places to go as an expat, to be fair. There's so much set up for you to do. You could join social clubs, go hiking with the English women, attend the American women's afternoon coffee clubs and lunches, or play golf with the Australians. There's a lot of variety. The English women at the time, they were really into doing the hiking and other outdoor activities, and I didn't really fancy that, so I just joined different groups. You didn't have to be that nationality, either. I also joined the YWCA, the Young Women's

Fitting In

Christian Assocation, though admittedly I didn't do much on the charitable side. They had a really good educational set up, which is why I joined. When you first move to Hong Kong, you could take this course called 'At home in Hong Kong', which I did. It was a couple of hours each week and it gave you the chance to meet a room full of women, often seven or eight different nationalities, who were all in the same situation as you. You'd then learn about how to find a doctor, that sort of thing. The things no-one really shows you how to do when you first move to a country. I met a really nice Australian woman there. She was a lawyer but had moved because of her husband's work, but it meant she couldn't practice law there herself. She really, really struggled with the mindset shift, unfortunately. I could see how you'd have a rough time if you didn't get that shift right. I used to joke to people that I was retired, that I'd given up working to move to Hong Kong. I wasn't actively looking for a job, so what do you call me?

Towards the end of my time in Hong Kong, I decided to do a degree with the Open University. I just did Social Sciences, so that was a little bit of sociology and a little bit of psychology. It was more just for interest, really. You can study for five or six years with them, and by the time I left the USA, I had a bachelor's degree. I thought, if I ever do want to get another job, then it wouldn't hurt to get a degree, but that wasn't the reason I started doing it. I just wanted to keep my brain going, I wanted to be thinking, I wanted to be doing something. I just picked something that was interesting to me, I guess. It really helped me structure the day, to give me a target by the end of the week. To finish reading chapters, to get to whatever point on the internet. It made me really focus and took away any guilt I felt about just going out during the day or alternatively if I was just staying home reading, as I was reading for the course. It made me feel good.

With being an ex-pat wife, my husband often needs to travel

for work. Sometimes I'd go along with him, and other times I'd just stay at home. It can be nice, that, too. You can treat it all like a bit of a holiday. Again, it goes back to your mindset. If my husband goes away for two weeks, I could sit around and be miserable. Alternatively, I could come up with a plan and go out and do things. I could get up and do something, then be home by 3pm, and in the bath with a face pack on, paint my toenails, watch whatever movie I wanted. All these things I never get a chance to do, I just do them.

DEAN - GERMANY

One of the things I missed the most after leaving England, was the football. It sounds stupid, doesn't it? There's football everywhere, but I did miss going to Sunderland games and being among all that on a Saturday. So, when I lived in Osnabruck for a few years, I started going to the football there. I was only there studying, but I said to a few mates that we should go down and watch the local team. It was only about nine euros for a student ticket, but one by one my mates dropped out on me. We'd have a big night on the Friday and people just never got to the game on the Saturday. I just figured I'd go on my own anyway, see what it was all about. So, I looked on the website, picked behind the goal as it was the cheapest area, and just went down there.

It turns out that I'd picked the ultras block and it was just full of lads jumping around like lunatics. It was pretty clear from the start that I didn't fit in. I didn't have a shirt, didn't have a scarf, wasn't wearing a hat, and wasn't singing any of the songs. After a while this guy comes up to me and asks who I am and what I was doing. I wasn't as confident back then with my German and this guy felt quite aggressive, at least I thought it at the time. It was just a German guy saying, 'So what are you doing here, then?', which is 'Was machst du dann hier?', if you translate it.

In English though, that comes across a bit aggressive. I felt like he was having a go, as you naturally would at a game in England. So, I just explained that I was English, that I lived in the city now, and that I missed the football. The next thing, he shouts up to the guy with the megaphone, the one leading the crowd at the front, and announces that there's an English guy here who doesn't know the words. By this time, I'm just stood there thinking, 'Oh shit, what's happening here?' and, no word of a lie, they passed this book down full of song lyrics so I could join in. It's an experience I'll never forget, for sure.

Then when I first moved to Ingolstadt, I didn't have a season ticket here, but I went to a couple of games with some lads. When we're talking about FC Ingolstadt, or Die Schanzer as they're known, everyone's into it and the chat is good. However, try to talk about other football here, and people aren't into it like they are back in England. For my friend's back there, the Champions League Final is the pinnacle of football every year for us. None of our teams are ever in it, and Sunderland are never going to be there, but we'd still always make plans and make it a big occasion. We'd head out to a bar, go round someone's house, that sort of thing. Here? You ask people if they're watching the game at the weekend, but if Bayern aren't in it, then they're just not interested. I remember the Madrid versus Juventus final a couple of years ago, my Spanish friend from Munich had to come up just to watch the game because neither of us could find anyone locally. Football and the way it can engage society, it's definitely different in England.

The thing is though mate, as much as I miss that football culture, I wouldn't swap my time in either Barcelona or my different spells in Germany. Living in mainland Europe, getting to really know new countries and ways of living, it's been great and a big part of who I am. And while I quite like being the foreigner here at times, I've always tried to throw myself into this place and I think speaking the language is a big part of that. Don't get me wrong, people can make you feel incredibly welcome when you don't speak the language here, but the only one missing out will be yourself. The idea of waiting for people to translate day to day conversations, that really got on my tits personally, so I adapted.

There's this phrase, that you can get by, isn't there? But if I'm living somewhere, I don't want to just get by. I want to immerse myself in that way of life, just like I would if I was living in the UK. I don't buy into the idea that it's rude not to learn the language, but you're only hindering yourself if you don't. The goal, for me at least, should be full integration, and I love it when people think I'm German now. It's a tick in a box or a goal achieved, I suppose.

HELEN – NORWAY

My Dad worked for an American pharmaceuticals company, and because of his job we lived in both Belgium and Norway when I was younger. I had really good memories of living in Norway, too. I was at that golden age just before you're a teenager, around ten or eleven, and before everything gets complicated in life. You'd have no conflict between friends and family, no real responsibilities, and everything just seemed so idyllic to me then. However, we're all English, and we came back to England when I was twelve and carried on life there. It's not until I went to university and was then introduced to a Norwegian on the premise that I'd once lived there, that I'd even thought about the country again. There were seven other Norwegians at the whole university, apparently, so the chances of me meeting my Norwegian partner there weren't that high, either.

We'd lived in London after university but ended up moving out to a countryside village with my job. The problem was then that I'd travel a lot for work and my partner was at home. He was bored in the middle of nowhere and away from his friends, so he was really keen to move back into a big city. At that point, we couldn't afford to buy anywhere in London, so we talked about cities up North, or up in Scotland, or in different parts of Europe. Then, we were at a Halloween party at one of my friend's and after a few drinks, I just said, 'Well, we could go to Norway.' Despite being Norwegian, he still thought that Oslo was a bit small and probably a bit too parochial for him, but I managed to convince him. So, on that whim, we started applying for jobs out here and agreed that we'd move when one of us got one. He got a job first, we moved, and fifteen years later we're still here, still married, and now have two children.

The stereotype of Norway being an expensive place to live, it is true. While it is expensive here, the salaries are much higher too. Just think, if you want to buy a flat in a nice central area of London, your salary alone probably isn't enough. You'd have to be lucky with inheritance, I think. It's either that, or you live miles out and spend hours commuting every day. When we bought a flat here in 2005, it was manageable on just two graduate salaries, without a deposit, too. Every capital city has a quarter that once used to be Jewish, then it's a working-class quarter, then it becomes a student and bohemian area, and then it gentrifies. That's where we managed to buy a flat here, and I suppose it would've been the equivalent of somewhere like Notting Hill back in the day. It was a dream for us, we found somewhere that just wouldn't have been accessible in London at the time. You still have these Facebook groups where British people are constantly comparing the price of Crunchy Nut Cornflakes, which are seventy-five krone or about £6.50 by the way, but they aren't often comparing the salaries at the same time.

Something I really appreciate in Norway, is the work-life balance. It's also one of the reasons why I've never seriously considered moving back. Here, you've got a shorter working day, family is really prioritised, and you've got so many more outdoor activities for your free time. It's totally unacceptable for people to work themselves to the ground here. I'm at home when the kids eat breakfast, I work a full day, and then I'm home for them to have their tea. With that, I can still go out for a jog, or we can go to the park and have an ice cream. I just feel it's much easier to balance work and free time, even though we live in a capital city. I know I couldn't do that in London without having to spend money on help, things like nannies and childcare.

Emigrating here, or just being foreign here, has become less novel for the locals over the years. They've still got a way to go before they're completely open-minded to foreigners, but it's improving. They do think it's charming that someone would choose to live here, too. They're very self-deprecating and often can't believe that someone would willingly choose to live in their peripheral, cold, and expensive country. Although inwardly they're really proud of it and do like when people come in, learn the language, try to integrate themselves, and call it their home. So, things like going cross-country skiing, ice skating, embracing the outdoors in the dark and cold months, that'll go a long way. That's definitely one way to fit in there, to enjoy the same things they enjoy doing. You can't go to the same ex-pat pub every day or stay indoors moaning and expect to enjoy life, can you? Embracing typical Norwegian leisure activities makes me happy and helps me really enjoy the best sides of life in Norway.

I once read a blog from a Canadian that said as soon as you've lived in more than one place, wherever you then choose to live is a perpetual compromise. You can't get the best of everywhere in one place. So, you'll always be conscious of the things that you don't have in the place where you currently are. It's about getting that balance right between the compromise, working out what you miss and finding what you're happiest with. Looking back at what you originally had at home, that's a far larger part of your consciousness once you've lived elsewhere.

146

It's been fifteen years now, and you know what, I've stopped talking about moving back. For the first few years, people back in the UK would often ask me when I'd be moving home. I'd just say, 'I don't know, let's see.' I did quite like the idea of the children experiencing living in both countries, as they were born in Norway. But then, the years have gone by and it's never felt like the right idea. I feel happier with staying in Norway, although I do miss my family and friends. It's funny how things change. We never made plans to stay permanently, but it's just ended up that way.

CLAIRE – KUWAIT, SWITZERLAND, & NETHERLANDS

My husband was approached by a former colleague to work for a big brand in Amsterdam, and even though we'd never been to the Netherlands before, we went. We were sick to death of living in the Cotswolds, and probably ten years too young to have settled in the countryside. So, we decided to get the hell out of there. I'm glad we did, as we absolutely loved it in the Netherlands. We were living between Amsterdam and the beach, so it was quick to get to both places. It was just very outdoorsy in general and an amazing place to raise children. You could ride your bike everywhere, for example. I'd ride my bike to the beach after work, have a glass of wine, and watch my children play in the sand. It was a fabulous, fabulous lifestyle.

I did miss working at times as I had a lovely job back in England. It was focused on empowering women, helping people get back on their feet after going through traumatic times. We'd teach them skills and support them along the way. So, I missed that, but I just became more focused on getting my children settled. That became my job and my role for my family, and it's been that way since we left the UK.

The children were five and nine when we moved, so they were both at school. It felt hard for them at first, going to a Dutch school and not really knowing what was going on, but within six months they were fluent. From that point on, we really didn't need to worry about them. With my son, he has ADHD, and he's very much about his opinions, about being heard regardless of being a child, and so on. The great thing was that really worked in the Netherlands for him, and he just loved their style of education. People would listen to him and engage with what he was saying, so he absolutely loved it there and he really thrived. He's super confident in general, which really helped. My daughter is the opposite, though. She's shy, she's anxious, but she eventually found her friendship group, too.

In the Netherlands, we found it relatively easy to integrate ourselves. We rented for a year on the most perfect street in the world and the kids went to the local school, literally within a three-minute walk. So, they'd come out of school, skip down the street, and draw with chalk on the floor for hours. It was a really wholesome life for them. After that year, we got lucky as our neighbours sold their house to us without them needing to put it on the market. And before too long, we knew everyone in the area. Eventually, the Dutch were surprised we hadn't left and started to make friends with us. It was just lovely, it really was, and if you ask my children where their home is now, they'd both say the Netherlands.

However, and not for the first time in our story, my husband was offered an interesting job in another country, in Switzerland in fact. We've both moved our whole lives, so we thought we'd give that a go. We lived in a beautiful house on top of a mountain for two and a half years, and while that location was great, the locals never really felt as welcoming to me. Where we lived was quite ex-patty, admittedly, but it just always seemed like an 'Us' versus 'Them' situation. And while it's all very beautiful,

living in Switzerland could be a little boring at times. It didn't
help that I was driving the kids forty-five minutes each way to
school, either, but that was just what I had to do for them. The
difference with this move, was that the children were old enough
to have made lives for themselves in the Netherland, so pulling
them away from that was very difficult. Pulling my daughter
away from her friends, that was a real wrench.

By that stage, I started to have my own routine for wherever
we were going to live. I find my local yoga class, I find my local
language school, and I make sure the kids are happy at school.
Everything else just slots in around me from there. Being at
home, being the Mum, I've always been happy to do that. I'm
there to make sure the children have settled, I'm there to pick
them up exactly when I said I'd pick them up, and I'm there
to give them that sense of consistency. Children need that,
especially if you're moving around, and I've never had an issue
with being the Mum.

When our third move materialized, after my husband was
made redundant in Switzerland, it was a very different move. I'd
never been to the Middle East, let alone to Kuwait, and moving
here has certainly been an experience. As my son was old enough
by then, he stayed in Switzerland to work, so it was just the three
of us. I initially said we'd give it two years and if we didn't like it,
I'd expect my husband to consider moving again. It's been three
years now though, so it's working out okay.

The racism and the poverty here are very noticeable, I
have to say, and that's a big change from the Netherlands and
Switzerland. If you have any issue with your daily life here and
you tell someone, they'll instantly ask where the person is from.
'They're from Egypt? You can't trust them. Pakistan? No, they're
dirty,' they'll say. It seems like everyone instantly has something
to say about other nationalities, so I do often wonder what they
think about the British. And with the poverty, it makes you feel
very spoiled. We have a housemaid here, so we don't have to do

149

our laundry or anything domestic like that, and you get spoiled very quickly. Whereas many of the people in service jobs here, they're living in awful conditions and probably having shitty lives. I just try my best to be nice to everyone, to give them something positive to take from the day. It's the least I can do, really.

My life will always be dictated by my husband's job, though. If he has a shitty day and someone calls him and offers him a job somewhere else, then we could possibly be off again. We like moving though, and we're not tied to one place. People ask us where we're going next, but we really don't know yet.

PAUL – SAUDI ARABIA

The thing is, back then I wasn't initially looking to leave England. My brother and sister both had opportunities at one stage or another, and I remember saying to them, 'Why the hell would you want to leave England?' It didn't make sense to me. I felt like it was a country of great ambition, great opportunities, and it was really changing for the better. I was flying in the executive world at the time, though. I was one of the youngest managers in the company, my boss was one of the youngest at his level, and we were absolutely flying together. So, thinking of leaving? No, that wasn't for me. I guess, and I'm not too proud to admit this, I didn't see that changing. But it did. Eventually, by the time I was recruited for this job in Saudi, I was completely fed up with life in the UK and being in the country was just killing me. The economic landscape had changed, I was getting dragged down by a 16% mortgage rate, and my house was in negative equity. I'd worked myself into a situation where I was taking home less than I owed each month, which wasn't great, and it couldn't really go on. By the time I left for the Middle East, I was in significant debt and just desperate to try something else.

Fitting In

The idea at the time, was that they wanted English guys with automotive experience to go out to Saudi Arabi and help them run the business. They felt it gave them some credibility and that we'd take a great deal of knowledge out there with us. And they're right, too, that definitely did help at times. The thing is, they'd also warned that we'd have to buy into the culture and the way of life in the country to make it work. As a result, they said that often people stay for two weeks, two years, or they'll become a lifer. Well, out of the three of us, one guy left after two weeks, the other guy lasted nine months, and I ended up there for twelve years. So, I was well on my way to being a lifer at that point. I guess the difference for me, was that I really tried to integrate, to tolerate, to understand the local way of life, and to learn as I went along. It wasn't always easy, and I definitely didn't get it right straight away, but I made it work.

Saudi Arabia was extremely strict and very religious when I moved there, and it still is today in any many ways. And when you're running a business there, you had to learn to deal with the five prayer times a day. It would be half past twelve, half past three, half past five, and so on. That means you close down for forty minutes at a time while everyone prays, has a wash, gets a coffee, and then goes back to work. As I'm not a religious man myself, I had to close my blinds and stay in my office during this. Imagine trying to run a business with that? You also had to deal with Ramadan, which was new. In the first year, I thought I'd just run my business rigidly, not military, but rigidly, and that was the way to do it. Eventually, my boss pulled me to one side and said I needed to calm down a bit, that my guys weren't eating, weren't drinking, didn't smoke during the day, and just didn't have the energy to function in the same way. He said the sales would still come, but I had to be more patient. That really made me take notice, though. The following year, I ran the business in the exact same way, only this time, I joined them in the fasting. I realised that if I wasn't willing to make a sacrifice and join them, how could I expect them to do more for me. They definitely respected me for that, and my boss was right, the sales did come.

You'll often hear of people who expect their new country to change for them, but it's obviously not how it works, and definitely not in the Middle East, either. You could try, of course, but the way I made it work was by just keeping my mouth shut, understanding what it was all about, and just allowing others to live their own lives. Of course, following their rules and traditions didn't have to extend to my private life or when I was traveling, so I was still able to have that release. We'd live in these compounds, for a start, and inside those you'd have a load of ex-pats like us. And I'll tell you what, we brewed and drank more beer there than I've ever had in my lifetime. So, it might be a dry country, but you could make it work in a respectful, behind closed doors way. You know when you hear your grandparents talking about how in their day, they used to get the piano out and have a really good night? Well, it was exactly like that for us, too. We'd have a great time. It was just all about creating your own entertainment and not flaunting that at the locals.

SETTLING DOWN

LEE – NETHERLANDS

I was back in Newcastle, working in the store there, and the trainee manager I was looking after, this Polish guy, he told me he was moving to Rotterdam for work. It was going to be the first store we'd opened in Northern Europe apparently and to me it sounded like a great opportunity. I looked at him and said, 'You know what, I'm coming with you.' Of course, he thought I was joking at the time. I was just starting to go through a divorce in my private life though, and this seemed like a great way for me to escape. So, the next day, I went in and asked for a transfer.

What many people didn't know at the time, was that my grandfather was Dutch. In fact, my middle name is Jan, which is a Dutch name. So, in addition to having that escapism, I thought this was a good chance to see a bit of me heritage, I suppose. Back then, my grandfather was in the Second World War and he was on one of the last ships that left the Netherlands. It was hit though, and they ended up stopped on the Tyne in Newcastle and he couldn't speak a word of English. That's where he eventually met me grandmother, and in typical Dutch fashion

153

he ended up making her pregnant and got married to her after the war. That's not the only connection, either, as his brother, so my great uncle, he was a pilot in the war. The Luftwaffe were scouring the country looking for these people, but he'd managed to escape to Amsterdam. Once there, he apparently dressed up as a woman and hid with the prostitutes for the rest of the war. He was a real cad, and I can imagine him having a whale of a time during that war. So, anyway, I had a connection to the Netherlands already and I just thought I'd give it a go. I moved in with the Polish guy and another friend, and we were set.

I was thirty-three at the time and it was a little bit of an adventure for me, really. I thought initially that I'd be here for a year, I'd enjoy it, and then I'd go home and have something to tell my friends and family about. I never expected to spend eleven years here, but I was having a great time with my friends and it just went from there. To start with though, I was a little bit lost at times and probably homesick. One day, another friend, he gave me some really good advice. He said, 'Every time you walk out that door Lee, you turn left. Why don't you just turn right one time and see what's there?' He was right, too. I took that on board and really started to see more, to do more things, to give it a proper go out here. Then there's me Mam, who was terrified of the idea at first. She came over to the Netherlands, spoke to my friends, and soon realised I wasn't up to no-good. She could see I wasn't taking drugs, paying for prostitutes, nor had I become this disease-ridden fella. She said she was relieved. I remember taking her up to Amsterdam, showing her the sights, and then on the way back on the train I asked her if she was happy now. She said, 'I'm relieved, son. I know you're going to be alright.' From there, the years have just rolled into the next, really.

I quickly met a girl, Kelly, who's now my wife. We were friends, and I was probably too old for her if I'm honest, but it ended up developing into something else. I did say to her initially that I'd stay while she finished university and then we'd go back to Newcastle together, and that was our intention for a few years. I kept thinking to myself, 'Well, I'm going home soon.' By the time it came round, I had a great job, a nice house, I lived by a lake. I just thought to myself, 'Why am I even thinking about this?' Sure, I missed me Mam, missed me Dad, missed me brother, but I'd never get what I had here back in Newcastle. I loved this country, loved this city, and just felt a real kinship with the Rotterdammers, too. My wife's a real Rotterdammer, and we've now got a five-year-old girl, who's also a real Rotterdammer. So, it's been great for me, this city.

ROBERT – CANADA

My relationship with Canada started shortly after leaving university and I've been back and forth since. Back then, in the '80s, I wrote a research paper about energy conservation in the paper manufacturing industry. I'd written a really favourable comment in it about this Canada company, one based in Vancouver, and I thought I'd send it to them to see what they thought. They seemed to love it, so much so that they invited me to the country for six months to work with them. They couldn't offer me a paid job, as I wasn't eligible for a working visa, but they covered my accommodation and gave me a meal allowance. The cool thing about that time, was that I was working in a lab for them and getting to fly across the province of British Columbia collecting tree samples in a float plane, one of those that could land on water. I had my pilots license, you see, having been in the navy cadets, and it was great fun. The idea was that I'd fly out somewhere, chop trees down, and bring the samples back to the lab. I was twenty-two at the time and I spent that six months flying these planes during the day, and then hanging out at night with a group of nurses that had also moved to the city at the same time. It was a classic post-university party, really.

After that, I headed back to the UK and studied to be an accountant. Not as exciting, I admit. Once I'd gained the qualifications, I started working for a well-known company, one of those international corporations who have offices across the world. They were offering secondment programmes at the time, and I jumped at the chance to move back across to Canada, but this time to Toronto. If I'm honest, I lived a pretty bog standard, boring ex-pat life. You could feel really isolated at times doing that, as it was long before the internet and smart phones, but I still enjoyed it. My only real connection back to England, was when I'd call my parents at the same time every single week. That was it. It was a brief call, too, as it cost so much. The difference with this stay, was that I fell into several ex-pat community groups and really settled into the place in general. I was friends with South Africans, Australians, Brits, and obviously Canadians, too. I also ended up meeting a Canadian, getting married, and eventually applied for Canadian citizenship. It was relatively easy to do so back then, you just needed a degree, the ability to speak English, and have a professional qualification. So, I thought, 'Why not?' The hilarious thing was that you had to pledge allegiance to the Queen, which wasn't too difficult for an Englishman, exactly.

Eventually, my Canadian wife and I moved back to the UK, after my work at the time asked if I could. The difference was that I came back to England as a Canadian citizen, so I was technically an ex-pat again, just the other way round this time. Unfortunately, we ended up getting a divorce. We had a child together, a boy, but he suffered an injury that no-one spotted while being born and ended up being severely disabled as a result. He tragically died when he was ten, which was a pretty horrific experience. We weren't really the same after that, as you can imagine.

I then spent a fairly long period back in England, living and working in Berkshire for about the next sixteen years. I met an

Settling Down

English woman this time, married her, and she's still my wife today. So, for some people, that Canadian experience might've ended there, back in England with an English wife. With me though, I was still traveling across to Canada for work, taking me back to British Columbia a few times. While I was there, it reminded me how much I loved the country, and how fabulous I thought it was. And with having the right to live and work there, I just really wanted to give it a go again. So, for the third time, and currently the last planned time, I ended up back in Canada and that's where I'm talking to you from right now. I have a five-month-old daughter here with me, too, which has certainly been a bit of a change for me.

I absolutely love living in Canada, I really do. It's such a supportive, considerate, and welcoming place. I find people are happy to help each other out, to give you confidence when you need it, and I really don't think that happens in the same way in the UK. Sure, there are millions of nice people there, but I don't get that same sense of the collective or rallying around to help people. A great example of that is from about two years ago. I was walking along the seawall here in Vancouver, this beautiful place near the beach, and I spotted this couple that had obviously just got married. You could just tell that they didn't have any money, as he had a suit on that was about five sizes too big and was wearing trainers, and she had this wedding dress on that really didn't fit her. They looked happy, really sweet, and very much in love, though. I watched them trying to take a selfie on their iPhones, just on the beach, and it was cute, but I thought they deserved more. So, I went up to them and said, 'Give me five minutes, I've got a really nice camera, I love photography, and I going to come back and take some photos.' So, I ran home, got the camera, ran back and found ten people around them. There was a guy who was a make-up artist, as there's a big movie industry here, which is funny as this does sound like a scene from a movie, doesn't it? Then there was another guy who was a hair stylist. There was someone there with a collapsible light reflector, and there were five guys with cameras. These were just random people walking past, seeing a life event and wanting to make it better for the couple. It was awesome and something that's really stuck with me since. That sums up this place for me, it really does.

TOM - JAPAN

I came to Japan on a whim after university, really. My girlfriend at the time had studied Japanese when she was at high school, weirdly enough, and had spent two weeks at a homestay here as a result. She seemed to love it by all accounts, so much so that she wanted to find a way to come back once she'd graduated from university. After looking around, she found this programme where you could work as a teaching assistant in a Japanese high school for a year or so. I think she saw it like a gap year, something to do before going back home and getting a proper job, that sort of thing. The thing is, I didn't really know what to do with myself back then, but I just thought I'd apply for it, too. I knew nothing about the country, and said as much in the interview, but I somehow managed to get a place in Osaka. So did my girlfriend. Apparently, couples do apply, but it's rare that they're both successful and extremely rare for them to end up in the same city. So, that seemed pretty cool and I was happy to go along with it.

When you accept one of these teaching assistant jobs, you find out about it in dribs and drabs from your predecessor. You effectively move into their old apartment and take their job, too. So, they were sending me emails about their life, telling me about the local area, and giving me some insights into the school I'd be working at. For me, that's when it really started to get interesting. When arriving here though, I found the Japanese schools a little weird, and I still do, really. The buildings are these grey, drab concrete blocks, but the kids just seem to love being here. They're here after school, at weekends, and even during their school holidays. They just absolutely love it. It's debatable whether they come out of it with a better education, but it's certainly a more rounded one. They seem to learn a lot about world history, classical music, famous artists, and things like that. I don't remember learning things like that in high school. Their English isn't very good, though. I was helping teach fifteen- to eighteen-year-olds initially, who'd been learning the language for years, but you wouldn't be able to tell that. Japan is famous for their poor English education, though no one seems to have worked out why. Hopefully it's not just my inability to teach them, though.

Despite everything feeling a little alien to me when I first moved here, I settled down eventually and have felt comfortable here since. I extended my stay to a second year, then stayed the full five years of my visa, and have since racked up twelve years quite quickly. I didn't see that coming, but it just felt like home here and I didn't see any reason to change that again. My girlfriend didn't stick around for long, though. Within six months she knew she wanted to go back, she felt homesick and just wasn't enjoying it. She lived in a grotty part of the city, a built-up area near the main station, one surrounded by businesses. Her apartment was awful, too. It was just this tiny little room. She also didn't really like working at her school and had a few issues there. So, it was all just too much, and she left before the end of her one-year contract. Our relationship was fizzling out by then, and had been for a while, so she went back home, we broke up, and I stayed here.

I didn't really feel that attracted to Asian women before I lived here. Even a year into life in Japan, I don't remember even considering it. I know quite a few foreigners come over here looking to get into relationships with them, but it just wasn't on my mind. After a while, I gradually started finding them attractive, had a few Japanese girlfriends, and then I met my wife. It's interesting, that dynamic, as some Japanese families are weary about having a foreigner enter the mist and it can cause issues. My wife's family are very traditional, they don't speak a lick of English, but they've always been fine with me.

We have a child now who is half British, half Japanese. We're trying to bring him up to be bilingual, but that will be quite challenging when he's surrounded by Japanese every day. I'll only be speaking to him in English, though, and I'll see if that helps. There aren't many kids with dual nationalities in this area, but you do sometimes hear horror stories about how they struggle to conform in schools, but I think he'll be fine. I've worked in a school for twelve years now and I genuinely don't see any bullying here. On the flip side, dual nationality teenagers are becoming quite popular. There're several famous Western celebrities here, too, so the younger generations are opening themselves up to that idea. I'm not going to force my son into anything he doesn't want to do, but I've love him to grow up and be a player for Cerezo Osaka. That'd be cool, right?

SONIA – GERMANY

I was born and raised in England, but with an English father and a German mother. So, despite feeling very English as a child, there was always that side of me that was a touch different. From that upbringing though, I could speak the language relatively well from an early age and went on to study it at school and university. I figured why complicate things by studying French as my foreign language, if you know what I mean. And from that degree, I got the chance to spend a year abroad and ended up in Nuremberg. I initially had no idea where that was, but I heard my best friend was already going there and I just put it down as my preferred choice. It was great, though, and I'll always be glad that I came here. It was initially just for that year, after which I went back home and finished my degree.

Back at university, I kept hearing from other language students about these great times they'd had across Europe teaching English. I felt like I'd missed out a little, as Nuremburg was great, but it wasn't this exciting, lively place exactly. So, I decided I'd sign up for teaching English abroad and find out what I was missing. I ended up in Berlin, which has always been a city I've loved. Living there, fresh from university, was amazing. You're curious at that age, you're ready to go out, meet new people, really get into the nightlife. And that nightlife in Berlin, that's really played a huge part in why I loved living there. It's also a city where, even today, everyone can be who they want to be. You can pick five random people off the streets there, and they'll all be different, but they all fit in. I don't think you necessarily find that elsewhere. The problem was that I didn't really like the teaching part enough to continue with it. I had planned to spend a year doing that, then go back to university in Manchester to study teaching. But doing that for a year, that was enough for me. So, just to tide me over for a bit, I moved back to Nuremberg and got myself a job. Within six months, I found another job at the company I'm still working for today, twenty-four years later.

Living in this country for twenty-five years, that sounds like an unbelievable amount of time when I think about it. Not in a negative sense, of course, but that's more than half my life. I only planned to be here for a year, too. The thing is, it's gone incredibly quickly, and I've enjoyed all of it. I've got everything I wanted in life here, too. I'm married, I've had my children, I've liked my career. I've also loved living in Bavaria. The Bavarians think they're special, of course, but there are some very special things about this place. It's a beautiful part of the country, overall. You've got the mountains, the beautiful lakes, the nice

161

weather, it's all very good. So, I've never really had a reason to leave here or to return to the UK.

While living here has always been straightforward for me, especially with speaking the language, I can sometimes feel a little lost in myself. I often feel like I'm neither English nor German now, but that I'm somewhere in between, really. It sometimes feels, to me at least, like everyone else around me knows where they belong and that they happily fit into this one place, with one home, with one clear identity. Whereas for me, I'm somewhere in between. I'm neither here, nor there, aren't I? Germany might physically be my home, but I have this English feeling inside me and that can be quite unsettling. People often ask me if I could choose one, what would I choose? Am I more English, or am I more German? I've never been able to quite answer that, though. It throws me off balance a little. So, at times I find myself having this identity crisis. I don't think I'm alone in those thoughts, I think it's something that a lot of people can question when they're living in another country.

They say, 'Home is where you heart is,' don't they? I think that's true. If you like where you're living, like the job you're working in, enjoy the people you spend your life with, then that's your home. It doesn't always have to be where you come from.

DAVID – BOSNIA AND HERZEGOVINA & AFGHANISTAN

I've loved radio since I was a kid. My friends and I used to listen to pirate radio during those four and a half golden years before the government shut it down. We were pissed off about that, so we started our own station. There were no more pirate radio stations on boats, and they wouldn't have taken sixteen-year-old boys without experience, anyway, so that was our best option. Eventually though, I joined the army as an apprentice and went off around the world with them, so left all that behind.

Throughout that time though, I remained fascinated by the radio and loved everything about it. I think the spoken word, such as podcasts or radio stations, are so much more effective than video. What audio has that video doesn't, is that audio is the theatre of the mind. You can paint a picture while reading a book, such as how the characters look or dress, and that's the same with the radio. You can be as ugly as sin on the radio, too, but if you have the voice then you can paint that picture for people.

So, with radio on my mind, after twenty years in the military, I stepped out and went to work for British Forces Radio. That's not staffed by soldiers, by the way, which people often don't realize. Unfortunately, I became unemployed there and despite vowing never to return to the army, I ended up joining the territorial army and was sent off to Bosnia. I'd been here before, back in 1993, and that was a really traumatic time. It was awful to see first-hand what human beings were capable of doing to others. It really was shocking and upsetting. So, when I returned years later, I wanted to find a way to bring people together, especially young people from different nationalities and backgrounds, so I set up a radio station and ran that for five and a half years.

I was blessed to be working with these multi-cultural young people in Bosnia. They were all under twenty-five when I started the radio station, and they just really defied the stereotypes that their politicians and leaders had put onto them. We have three distinct ethnic groups here, and they were all represented in this group of young people I was working with. We'd use the local language too, so we were using Serb-Croatian or Bosnian-Croatian. It's always important that. If you're trying to influence people to be more tolerant or see the world in a less violent way, then that should be conveyed in their own language. We would still have sections in English though. For a start, it helped if I could occasionally do a show myself and allow people to learn from me. But another big reason was that sponsors, whether military or NGOs, are often dubious about what you're saying if they can't easily follow you. So, throwing in English sections, that would always satisfy them and allow them to listen to the odd show.

It wasn't just Bosnia that I ended up doing this in, as I then spent time in Canada, in Kosovo, in Ethiopia, and in Afghanistan. In some of the more disputed regions, there was always a tremendous amount of opposition on these projects. They didn't like people from outside coming in and putting their views across in the area. In Afghanistan, for example, that was a very difficult area. You have these different ethnic groups, and they can be quite tribal. And in the main, the areas we were working in have seen full on anarchy breaking out at times. You also have a lot of opposition from governments, too, which is not that surprising. The way I dealt with that, was to find a specific type of young, local people to help me. I think younger people are the best as they still have a certain degree of rebelliousness inside them. They're willing to try and paint that bigger, brighter future, I think. And you know, there's something about going to help people, and trying to do that in a way that no one else has done, that's exciting. It's changed my view of the world, as a result. I'm less rosy eyed than I was before.

One day, I woke up in Kabul and we'd had a rocket attack from the Taliban, and the joke just finally wore out. The feeling you get when you leave is often, why did I do it? Did I make a difference? Will many people care when I leave? I just care if I've managed to do something. Eventually I found my way back to Bosnia. If you meet a lot of the Brits that live here now, regardless of whether they've married a local girl like I have, they'll say the same thing. If Bosnia and Herzegovinian bites you, you'll never want to leave. I've travelled the world, yet I have no desire to leave here now. There's a real majesty about this country. I often find areas or people that are just fascinating. There's just so much to see and understand here, and I'll never be an expert. Like with a game of snakes and ladders, just when I think I get what makes these people tick, I slide right back to the bottom. That's what makes every morning worth waking up to, knowing that I'll learn something.

This country is still dysfunctional, and they're as corrupt as anything. It has three languages, two entities, three presidents, thirteen different prime ministers, and eighty percent of its GDP pays for the politicians' salaries. It's totally corrupted. Yet, with all that, it's still somewhere where every day feels like an adventure. Getting out and seeing this country, experiencing its hospitality for the first time, it's a complete shock. They are so hospitable, so friendly, so welcoming. To see families, to hear their stories, it's amazing. To travel around a country like this with its eight micro-climates, it's just beautiful. You have the people, and you meet their families, you see their country, and you learn how they are. Their families are everything to them, and you find it hard to leave that. Why go back to the hustle, bustle, and crush? Why would I want to leave here?

FRAM – CANADA

About a month into my stay, I went to see my family in Toronto for Canadian Thanksgiving, and that's when I truly fell in love with the country. In addition to my grandparents surprising me for my birthday, as they'd come over for a medical conference in the city without telling me, we went on this great road trip down to Niagara Falls. That afternoon, we went to this beautiful town down the road called Niagara on the Lake. It has these quintessential Ontario stone brick buildings, crenellated roofs, and these big oak trees with their leaves turning orange and red in the Fall. It was a warm sunny day, and we were walking through the leaves on the floor and admiring the Halloween decorations on a few of the houses. It was really neat. On the drive back, we went through this forest and you could see the trees stretching through to the horizon and it was all lit by the setting sun. It was like an ocean of red, orange, and yellow, and I just remember looking across the landscape and thinking, 'I've come home. Canada is going to be my home.' I just had an epiphany of sorts. I just knew that this was the country I wanted to spend the rest of my life in.

Unfortunately, I couldn't instantly act on those feelings as I had to go back and finish my course. Leaving really upset me, too. I felt like I was leaving behind people that had made the experience so great, and I honestly felt like I was leaving my spiritual home. On that flight back to London, when we were cruising East across Newfoundland, I remember just looking down at the Canadian coast, feeling Canadian in my heart, and promising myself I'd return. I went back, finished my degree, took a year off between my degree and my post-grad studies and went traveling all over the place. I went to Germany, some of Europe, in India, in Iran, across to the States, and then Brazil. After my undergrad, I decided that I wanted to get into journalism. I knew I wanted to go back to Canada and that I didn't want to spend the rest of my life in the UK. I knew Canada was the place for me because there were so many more opportunities, especially for younger people. There's much more personal freedom, too. We have more space. You can live in a nicer house, in a ranch, you can have the mountains as your backyard. You have an entire continent to explore at your feet. For me, that was a liberating experience, and I knew I needed to go back.

I got accepted into journalism school in Vancouver and so, almost three years later, I was finally on a plane back to Canada. The irony of thinking that there were more opportunities for the younger generation though, was that I graduated at the height of the recession in Canada. It ended up taking me a year to find a career job and, in the meantime, I worked part-time at my local Safeway to help make rent, as well as freelancing and working for free.

It was tough breaking into the industry, but my absolute worst point though came in 2015, working for a small-town paper in Alberta. One morning, I was called into the back office and fired. They said I wasn't growing as a professional. After a last-ditch effort on my part, they agreed to let me resign, but it did not change the fact I was so shocked and blindsided by this. It was an utterly humiliating experience, compounded by the fact that one of my ex-bosses there deleted me from her Facebook a few days later. I remember walking back home feeling like a complete failure. I remember calling up my Mum, as a thirty-year-old, and just being in absolute bits with her on the phone. I felt awful in that brief moment and very nearly said, 'Sod it, I'm coming home', but I was absolutely determined to make this work.

When you move abroad, part of you can't help but feel a failure if you don't stay. I'd have definitely felt like a failure if I had given up at any point. I made it very clear to my family and friends that I loved Canada, so to turn back on that would've been embarrassing. I think that's all part of being an ex-pat, though. You'll have those dark days, the ones where you wonder what the hell you're doing, but you'll then have some of your greatest successes in your new country at the same time.

As an example, soon after I left that job in Alberta, I started working for a new national outlet launched in Vancouver. I covered federal politics back then, working on the 2015 Canadian elections. On Election Day, I was at the Fairmount Hotel in Montreal, the headquarters of the Liberal party, and we camped out there on the night of the election. So, I was there livestreaming and liveblogging, getting streeters, getting videos, speaking to top-ranking Liberals, and getting reactions as results came in. It was the most exhilarating feeling and one of the most thrilling nights of my life. At about 9.40pm, the TV stations announced that Justin Trudeau was the winner. It felt like everything. People were standing up, clapping, cheering Trudeau's name like he was a footballer. There was mood lighting in the building, so it felt like being at Wembley when your team scores the winning goal in the FA Cup! Then at 12.30am, Trudeau comes on stage, and gives his victory speech. He was given a real rock star welcome. I wrote it all up, covered the story, got to bed about 2am, had about four hours sleep, but I was just running on fumes and adrenaline.

It was the real high point of my career, that. I witnessed history being made from a front row seat. I remember thinking to myself after, that there was no way I'd be doing something like this by staying in England. That kind of opportunity, that exposure, that kind of absolute thrill...that's what makes being in Canada worthwhile for me.

NICK – FINLAND, SAUDI ARABIA, & GERMANY

I was out of the UK for six years originally, working for the army out in Germany. I ended up joining them to straighten out my life, as it were, but it's not like anything was going particularly wrong for me at the time. I lived a very squaddie experience there, though. We were surrounded by the same people, all did the same stuff, and it left me with very little exposure to the country itself. I wouldn't say I was a typical squaddie, largely because I was working in medical operating theatres, but I certainly never lived out in the wider community or saw a great deal of it. What I did see I really liked, enough for me to head to Frankfurt for work once I'd left the army.

I've never classed myself as being particularly English or British, despite being in the army. It was where I was from, but it didn't define me as a person. And living in Frankfurt, I'd say I was an immigrant more than anything. I lived a German life, in a German city, while working a German job, and with Germans for friends. I didn't have this big ex-pat community that I slotted into or anything like that. So, yes, I was and still am English, but I've never felt the need to make much more of it.

From there, I ended up in Saudi Arabia and continued to work in hospitals. Obviously, that sounds like quite a departure for some people, but it worked for me. It's in Saudi Arabia where I met my wife, a Finnish lady, as she was working out there, too. We moved to just outside London for eighteen odd years after that. She was this mad scientist and worked in medical laboratories, whereas I was doing more clinical work myself. We did the usual commuting thing, lived in a couple of difference places, and felt very settled for a long time. After having our son though, and with her Finnish parents getting on a bit, we took the decision to move back to her home. Not only was she missing her Finnish roots a bit, but it gave my son a chance to grow up closer to his family. I didn't mind moving, either. I had no real close family connections left in England, so was happy to give Finland a go.

We live up North in a small village, very small in fact. I didn't mind that at first, but after a while you can feel a little cut off from the rest of society. It's about an hour and a half to the nearest city and even then, that city only has about fifty-thousand people in it. On the journey there, you'll pass a few houses on the road and very little else. There's literally nothing at times. It's either always been sparsely populated, or people just leave to go to the bigger cities. There are also huge areas here, bigger than whole countries, where you'll find absolutely no-one at all, it's that remote. There is a growing tourist industry up here, however. You used to find the Finns from the south would come up north for skiing, fish the rivers, that sort of thing. But then we started to get plane loads of Chinese tourists, as apparently Lapland is increasingly on their bucket lists.

I didn't know any Finnish before I arrived, but I didn't really have much choice. Although you'll see statistics that say things like eighty to ninety percent of Finns can speak English, it's just not true. There's a massive difference between taking it in school for a few years, and actually speaking the language, isn't there? I can't really complain, as I knew I needed to pick up the language here, but I can find their attitude to it quite surprising. You see, they're very officious here and they like you to take courses. They treat it almost as if you're deficient in something and a course will fix that. So, I took my Finnish lessons, and now I have a piece of paper that says I can speak and write Finnish. Yet, I've noticed that if my pronunciation isn't right or I'm struggling for the word, the locals here act as if they simply can't understand anything of what I'm saying. You're either entirely right or you're completely wrong, there's no in-between. It can make me feel incredibly self-conscious at times, like I've inconvenienced someone.

Since moving here, I've been looking after the English-speaking bit with my son. Part of that is to make sure that he doesn't grow up in this Finnish bubble. It's a beautiful country and you do meet a lot of nice people here, but there's a bubble that they all live in. They have a small population but a unique language and culture to go with it, and they can be proud of that, don't get me wrong. But I often think that very few of them can see outside of that thinking and that way of life. When we live in a global society now, you do have to consider other nations and the way they think and act. You can't just look at your own country in isolation. Finland doesn't consider what's happening elsewhere, even in this day and age. So, we have this Finnish national ethos of waving flags of equality, fairness, honesty, reliability, that sort of thing. However, when I look at the headlines or what goes on around me, Finns are no more honest or dishonest than anybody else. They have corruption, they have domestic abuse, they have crime rates, they've got drug issues, alcoholism, and so on. Yet, the way that they represent themselves to others, it's that they think they're somehow above every other country. In fact, you have the same issues as everyone else here. If the population was bigger, to the same ratio as other countries, you'd end up with more issues, I think.

SCOTT – JAPAN

I came to Japan straight from university in 2008, so it's been twelve years now. I honestly thought I'd be here for a year or two, pick up some experience, learn the language, and then go back to the UK and find a career from there. Twelve years? I don't think anyone expected that, let alone myself. I'd be lying if I said I had this big plan before leaving, though. I studied English at university and had a vague idea that I wanted to be a writer or a journalist at some point, but that was it. Back then, we'd get presentations after university lectures from people recruiting for careers in roles like management consulting. I'd just completely tune out from them, really. I was twenty-one at the time, and the idea of careers like that just didn't appeal. Everyone else I knew seemed to be moving down to London to do something like that, but I really didn't feel like it. Unfortunately, I graduated during the financial crisis, so it wasn't a great time to be finding a job in any country, anyway.

It's not until someone suggested teaching English as a foreign language that I'd even considered looking into jobs in other countries. I checked it out on a whim really and went down to London for an interview. I really wasn't taking it that seriously at first, but the more it progressed, the more the idea sounded cool. The job I ended up getting was working in an English conversation school, which they call an eikaiwa here, in Osaka. It's different to working as an assistant in a high school, which is a pretty common path for people. This was more helping adults practice their English with a native speaker. I figured I'd studied English, I knew my grammar, so I'd probably be pretty good at it. I'd never been to Asia before, let alone Japan, but I was interested in Japanese movies at the time and the idea of matching the places I was seeing on screen with real life, that really piqued my interest.

When I arrived in Japan, I wasn't confident in my ability to meet friends or build a life for myself out there. Going straight from university, to living by yourself in a city you've never been to, and on the other side of the planet? That initially felt really isolating and would eventually end up dragging me back to the UK, I assumed. In fact, it ended up being the opposite. Working at this conversation school, I found myself meeting people just like me. And because of the mechanics of the job, as I'd be going to different schools every week and meeting people from all over the world, it ended up being pretty sociable and a fun place to work. If anything, it just felt like an extension to university, just in another country. It all made it far easier to settle, becoming comfortable going out, and stuff like that. I got really locked into the loop of living here. But the job itself, I ended up not really liking it after a while. It was fun for a year or so, then it just felt like I was constantly doing fairly dry work. Also, the way conversation schools work, is that you're not really allowed to speak the local language. You're basically there to be a mannequin and reply to people in English. As it was doing my head in to be surrounded by Japanese people but being unable to speak to them like a normal human being would.

From there, I worked in a shop for a while, just managing the stock for a brand. I'd sit out the back, re-stock t-shirts, that sort of thing. That was actually, I'll be honest, a great job. It did wonders for my Japanese, as I was talking to people every single day. I know it sounds like a backward step to some people, graduating and then working in a shop, but at the time it was great and, like I said earlier, I didn't have these grand plans and a place I simply had to be in my career. It was while working at that job though, that I found an advert for my current role. I'm a journalist here now, so it was at least related to my degree again.

Initially, it felt like I'd go weeks here without seeing another foreigner who I didn't already know. It made sense, though. I think it's something like 98% Japanese citizens, and then from the remaining 2%, most of them are Korean or Chinese immigrants. So, Western immigrants like myself are very, very proportionally rare in this country. Those percentages are changing, especially in Tokyo, but the country is still fairly closed off to immigration. There's definitely the occasional xenophobic practice that you'll walk into, but on the average day, it's extremely unlikely that anything bad will happen to you. It's things like finding an apartment that can be difficult. When I last looked for one, we found some that accepted pets but wouldn't accept foreigners. They'll often have this flat no foreigner policy, that's fairly common. It's because we're often seen as a flight risk, even if you've been here as long as I have.

I don't want to downplay the negative aspects of living in Japan though, as I do think it's much harder for women and particularly if you're black or an ethnic minority. My wife still likes it here, but she certainly has a different experience to me. I know there's lots of sexism in older Japanese offices, for sure, and you'll have women-only carriages at the front or back of the trains here. That's become a bit of a necessary part of commuting here, unfortunately. Violence is unlikely, but sexual harassment is more prevalent.

I could recite the opening chapter of a Lonely Planet guide to Tokyo and say all these generic things that I'm sure people have heard a thousand times, but they're all true. It's a huge place, and I don't think I'll get bored of this city. It doesn't mean I'll stay here forever, but if I'm going to put down roots anywhere, I can think of far worse places. I don't hold any resentment or negative feelings towards England, though. Staying here isn't an emotional backlash, I'm just being pragmatic and see this as my best option right now.

FACING CHALLENGES

SIMONE – INDIA

I always wanted to live outside of the UK as the weather is bloody awful there. So, when I was eighteen, I went to live in Israel as an au-pair. I ended up staying for five years, picked up some Hebrew, and enjoyed most of it. I'd often go to Egypt on holiday from there and I'd meet loads of people out there on the hippy trail. These were hardened hippies, people who'd been to places like India and other parts of South Asia, and that always inspired me. I've always found that hippy lifestyle and the clothes pretty appealing, to be honest. So, I knew I'd end up in India at some point. After returning to England, I met a guy there, had my son with him, and was relatively settled for a bit. We'd both always wanted to travel though, and with the idea to go to India at the back of my mind, we eventually decided we'd go out there for a holiday to see if we liked it. We sold everything before that, put what was left in a motorhome that we'd parked up, and just went out to see what it was like. We ended up loving it, came back and sorted out a few bits, and then returned to the country with our four-year-old son to live.

Goodbye Britain

After a few months in India, we ended up breaking up. We'd been together eleven years, but it didn't work out. We had a big row and I ended up walking out when he was asleep, with nothing but my son and the clothes on my back. I was just sat at the side of the road crying, and this guy came along, someone I'd seen locally as he ran a stall in the market, and he asked me if I was okay and wanted a cup of tea. I went back to his shared room, had a cup of tea, calmed down a little, and then he offered me the chance to go back to Kasmir with him. I had nothing at the time, so I said okay. The problem was that my visa had already expired, and I thought I wouldn't get through any border checks. He didn't think it was a problem, said that I'd be his woman, and no-one would bother us. So, he dressed me head to toe in a burka, and no one did speak to me. I should've known then, to be honest.

He was very attractive, I was very attracted to him, and we were married within a month. He said that getting married would allow me to stay in India, and that's what I wanted to do. The fact that I had rather a large bank balance at the time, that might've swayed things for him, but stupidly, it just all made sense to me at the time. I soon realized it was a bad decision. He became very jealous and very possessive. People used to look at me as a Western woman and just assume that he was my guide in India, rather than my husband. He'd make me walk with my eyes to the ground in case I made eye contact with another man, who he assumed that I wanted to fuck, no doubt. Then the violence started. I felt trapped, in fact I was trapped as the area we were living in became an island in the winter and you could only get to it by boat. I say boat, it was just a round thing made of bamboo. Anyway, I never looked for support at the time, I just felt trapped there. There was a time that a policeman came over, as I always had to register with them whenever I moved areas, and I was sat there with a big black eye from being smashed in the face with a torch. He asked if I was alright, and I just told

176

him I'd fallen over and hit my head. I was six months pregnant with my daughter at the time, which wasn't ideal.

Back then, my mum used to come over every year to visit me and stay in a nearby hotel, one with proper security and guards on the gate. She came over when I was giving birth and asked me if I wanted to go home. My Mum knew things weren't good between us. Initially I said no because I felt like I had to try and make the marriage work for the sake of my daughter. She accepted the decision but wasn't happy about it. She came back when my daughter was a year old and this time, she told me that she couldn't keep coming over, couldn't keep seeing me like that and then leaving me behind. So, she asked me again, and this time I said yes. She was there when it all kicked off, luckily. I was breastfeeding my daughter at the time, stood up by the door, and he just suddenly slapped me across the face. The bottom of his hand caught the top of my daughter's head and she started crying. That's when my blood ran cold, and I knew I needed to leave. I waited until he went to work, phoned my Mum, packed my stuff up, and she organized a taxi to pick me up. The guards on the gate of her hotel were given instructions to stop him entering, which they happily did as they don't like the Kashmiris in India. He wasn't allowed to come in.

The thing was, I fell in love with him and he fell in love with me. He was so scared that I'd leave him, and it was his reaction to that, the violence and the possessive nature, that ironically made me actually leave. Before I left, I met up with him, and he bought nappies for the baby and sweets for my son. He was crying, he said he was sorry, he kissed my mother's feet and apologised for what he'd done. She said that he was nothing but a piece of shit on the bottom of her shoe and wouldn't have anything to do with him. She'd moved to Spain by this point, so took me back there with her and I never saw him again. We kept in contact for a while, but it was always me phoning him. When my Mum put a stop to that, as it was too expensive to keep phoning India, I never heard from him again.

My mum really saved my life. She was my hero. She died about eight years ago now and I miss her every day.

MARTIN – THAILAND

I've always been a bit of a traveller; this is the seventh different country I've worked in. I left England when I was nineteen, kinda disillusioned with what was happening career wise. I got into timeshare and moved out to Portugal initially. Once you start that sort of traveling and realizing that there's more out there than your nine to five and your mortgage, you get the bug for it. So, I've done timeshare in Portugal and Spain. I've worked in tourist caves and call centres in Ireland. Worked on a campsite in France. Helped aboriginal children in Australia, and so on. I ended up here in Thailand, up in Udon Thani, after splitting up with my ex-wife while in Australia. We'd moved over there to give her career a kickstart, as she's Australian, but eventually we were reading off different pages. I was drinking a lot. She was eating a lot and putting on weight. I was getting obnoxious. Neither of us were doing anything about it. We just drifted apart. I left and went to the other side of the country, figured I'd just travel around, and I ended up in Thailand.

I actually got a job just outside of Bangkok, and two days before I was due to leave Australia, the guy just went cold. He didn't answer my emails or anything. I just went out on a one year working visa anyway, and eventually ended up in Udon Thani. It's near the border of Laos, the northern border. It's been a little crazy since that, mate. I met a Thai woman, didn't take precautions, she fell pregnant. I'm in a situation now that's not pleasant. I split up with her, my son's mother, and I'm going through an ugly, messy custody battle.

He's eight and a half now, my son, and we're very close.

Forgive me for getting emotional, we were very close, I mean. Unfortunately, the woman, she was always argumentative, snappy, always a nightmare, and I put up with it for so long because of my son. Once he was five, I said I couldn't take it anymore, said I'm sorry, but that I couldn't sit by and watch my son grow up with all that hate. I didn't want him growing up to think this was how the world worked. This is how problems in the world can perpetuate, for me. So, I said I couldn't handle this anymore, moved out, carried on paying her rent, her electricity, her internet, her water, I gave her money. She didn't like working. It gave her a good chance to sit around and do nothing. I also paid for both boys' education, as she had another son. In a nutshell though, she said no, said that she wanted me to get out of Thailand and never see my son again. I said no, that's not going to happen, and then she abducted my son and took him away for fifteen months. I didn't see him for fifteen months. I was at a school sports day and I got a call to say they were gone.

Prior to that, I'd actually taken my son away for a night and we stayed in a hotel. I'd already got legal advice and they told me I just had to send her a text to tell her, so I did that. However, when we got back home, she'd locked the doors, padlocked it shut so I couldn't get back in. Later, she called the police on me. Called the army, accused me of locking my son in an apartment, accused me of slapping him, not taking him to school, teaching him to drink beer and whisky. He was five years old at the time. Mate, these are just the sort of things that she'd do. From the UK embassy alone, there were one hundred and thirty-four cases of child abduction in Thailand at that time. It happens quite a lot. If you get the wrong woman here, well, I don't even know the word to explain it. I got a random phone call from a stranger, telling me she could show me where my son was. I rushed down to Bangkok, I found him, and it forced her hand and made her move back up here.

Unfortunately, she then got full parental rights, so she

could make the decisions about his schools and the like. That's dangerous though, I'll tell you! I've been through family court where I was awarded access rights, then to a second one where they gave her full parental rights but didn't take my access away from me, so I still have that. They told me I had to build up a relationship with my son again because he's been away from me so long. And you know, it's so sad. He told me that he misses me, that he thinks about me a lot, but he's scared. He's eight and a half years old, he's just in self-protection mode and he knows that if he doesn't talk to me, he won't get shit from his mum. There are times when I've backed off for a few weeks or months, because I don't want him to go through that. It's horrible, it's horrible man. It's the worst. I can't even explain it. No one should have to go through this.

The dream situation is that she finds a new boyfriend, re-marries, and buggers off and leaves him here with me. I sincerely worry about his future. She dropped out of school in the second year of secondary school. She's got a really low level of education and she puts no importance on it all. Education here in Thailand is absolutely massive. If you don't have money and education, and this is the thing here, you will end up selling food on the street and living hand to mouth. I'm seeing changes in him now that I know, ten years down the line, will make him someone I might not like. It's a horrible thing to say, but he'll have principles and morals that I'll struggle to deal with. I hope that's not the case though, I really do.

KATHERINE – JAPAN

I come from a bit of a mixed background, myself. I grew up in Stockport with a black Dad and a white Mum, for a start. My father is a transracial adoptee, who was adopted by a white Irish family in the Northwich area. And by the time I arrived, my parents had this friendship group drawn from a wide range of places – you had Barbadians, Pakistanis, Jamaicans, Caribbeans, Nigerians. All sorts, really. So even though I grew up in Stockport, which isn't traditionally that diverse, I was always around different nationalities and different cultures. Unfortunately, my Mum was an alcoholic and ended up splitting up with my Dad. It meant I was put into a foster home when I was ten years old. It wasn't ideal but having grown up on a council estate with a single parent, that time in foster care really taught me how a family could operate.

Having had that diverse upbringing, I always wanted to go out and explore the world as an adult. I'd also developed a real fascination with languages, which I think I got from my Dad, and that led me to the Japanese language. Perhaps not your first thought when picking up a foreign language, but there was an explosion of Japanese culture around that time, so the manga, the animation, the music, and that made it really intriguing for me. I ended up moving to London, picking up a job at a Japanese supermarket, and started learning the language and finding out about the culture there. I also thought I'd apply for a Japanese course at university. I didn't get in, though, so to give myself an extra edge, and to see if I could really cut it, I decided to go by myself, with very little money, to Japan for a year. You know, as you do. I went on a working holiday visa, and I had very little idea of what I was doing.

I rocked up there and quickly realized that I'd thrown myself into a very challenging situation. Not for the first time and definitely not for the last time, either. I flew into Tokyo, met the company who I booked the experience through, and started looking for a job with them. I remember looking over all these jobs and everything required a degree, a teaching qualification, or it paid way less than would ensure my survival. After realizing this, I went back to the hostel, sat on the balcony, took a deep breath and, excuse my French, but just said, 'Oh shit. What have

181

I done?' It took about two weeks of trial and error, mainly error, of searching for jobs and going out with others at the hostel until five in the morning, before I really came to terms with it. I also moved into my first apartment without checking it first, and there were cockroaches everywhere. They were everywhere. They were in the cupboards, in the sofa, on the tv, they were even in the freezer. One very vivid memory I have is propping open the bin lid with a broom and emptying an entire can of cockroach killer into the bin. Hearing some scuttling, then an entire bin load of little cockroaches crawled out of the bin and died on the floor. It was grim.

I'm very, very stubborn and even at this point, I hadn't thought about changing my flights or anything. I was just a little stressed, the jobs weren't there, and the math just wasn't adding up for me. So, obviously going home was a last resort, but it just never realistically felt like an option. It's a self-pride thing for me. I think ninety-eight percent of the things that I do, if I stick them out and I'm stubborn, if I think I've got to do something, then I'll normally see it through. It's for my own self-satisfaction, if anything. I don't want to admit defeat for myself. I've got plans, I've got goals, and I want to see them through. After those two weeks, I was terrified, though. I was running out of money as I hadn't found a job, and just went back to the office and cried my eyes out, told them I didn't know what to do. Fortunately, they managed to calm me down and then announced that they'd found a job for me. It was a hot spring hotel, in the middle of nowhere, about four hours away from Tokyo. It had free accommodation, free food, and I'd get paid, so it sounded promising. So, I packed everything up, left the cockroaches behind, and got on a bus early one morning.

I spent eight months there, and it was a great experience from a language and culture perspective. I was one of the only non-Asian foreigners there, and most people didn't speak English. That really helps you learn the language, having to deal with customers in their native tongue. Most of them would get my name wrong, though, I'd be called things like Casablanca fairly regularly. I had some really interesting experiences working there, though. Once, during Golden Week, which is a busy period in Japan, there were whispers going around that we'd have a huge VIP coming in. Eventually, my boss came to me and asked if I would be willing to put in some extra effort for a Prince of the Japanese Royal family, and at the time it was the brother of the Emperor. He was coming with his baby son, second in line for the throne, and the rest of the family and his friends. It was a bizarre experience, being asked to do Japanese karaoke with royalty and dancing in a drunken conga line.

That was my first experience of living abroad, and in the following years I picked up far more international experience. I've lived in Frankfurt, in Brussels, in Geneva, multiple times in China, and in South Korea, where I am today. It's been difficult at times, and I've had moments where I've had to sit there and really question whether I belong in these situations, too. Considering where I've come from, what I've done and not done yet in my life, did I really belong in some of these atmospheres and in these places? I'm really not sure, but I know I wouldn't have got to be in them if I had stayed in Stockport all this time.

SUSAN – EGYPT

It's been move, move, move with me. My father was in the army, you see, and then I eventually joined the army myself. As such, I've always been used to different sounds, sights, smells, and cultures. It's just always felt natural to me, that. The thing with the army, though, is that you're often a little cocooned in that military lifestyle. Your social activities often revolve around the base, so you don't always see outside of that. It's not like you're just flung into the deep end and find yourself in a different country, with different languages around you, and expected to swim. It's more like you've got one foot in, one foot out, which is much easier. Being in the army, that did give me this sense of wanderlust though, and I've never really shrugged that off. I haven't tried to, mind. That's what's taken me to Germany, to Egypt, and now to Saudi Arabia.

After getting divorced from my husband at the time, who I'd lived with in Germany, I was back in the UK running a successful business on my own. I've always been very good at that, always very happy to make something like that work. The thing is, I just got bored eventually and felt ground down by doing the same thing every day. I knew I needed to do something else. One day, I woke up, sold my house, sold my business, and moved into my parent's renovated barn house while I worked out what to do next. Really, that wanderlust I was talking about, that got the better of me. To start with, I thought I'd take myself off to Egypt for a diving holiday and then have a think out there. However, that two weeks became a month, then two months, and before you know it, I decided I was staying out there. It just felt like paradise, like absolute paradise to me. I had the ancient Egyptian icons all around me, there were loads of ex-pats, I had the diving in the sea, the sun, palm trees all around me, it was just fantastic. I completely conned myself, if I'm honest. I was swept away by it all. I couldn't see past the idea of the holiday, though. I wish I could, but I was so swept away by it all and decided I wanted to live there. I just had this feeling; I liked the people I was meeting and loved the place, so that was me sorted.

On my second night in Egypt, I went into a perfume shop and it was riddled with shrapnel holes from the Sharm El-Sheik bombing. The shop had just never had the money to repair all the glass, you see. There was Arabic music playing and I just fell in love with the whole atmosphere. I got chatting to the young man working there and asked if this was the proper Egypt, so to speak, and he just laughed at me. I went back a few times, and he agreed to take me out and see the proper Egypt. We visited his sister, stopped at someone's mother's house, and I really did see what the real country was like. It was a real shock to me. I know I sound like an idiot, but I was just looking around, and my white saviour complex kicked in. I'd been so preconditioned through my parents and the army to believe that the white people can just wander in and fix something, and I thought I could do that too. There's me with this full bank account, surrounded by poor people with no opportunities, and I genuinely thought I could help them. I do worry that I sound like an awful person, I know. It's just this automatic thought that came into my head. So, I decided that this was it. I was going to move to Egypt and I was going to spend my time there helping these people.

My plan was to help these young guys to get married and start a life, as they have a totally different set up there. In the UK, you get married and you build up your life from there. In Egypt, you need to have everything before you get married. The bride's family will often tell you what make and model of car you need, how many carats the ring should be, or how many ounces of gold it needs to weigh. The bride's family will often tell you which area, or even what street, you must live on. All these things must be sorted out before. The bride's family will pay for the kitchen and the bedding, but the rest all comes from the man. So, if you come from a slum, and your father is a day wage labourer, how the hell do you get married and move on in life? I knew I couldn't change the world, or a city, or even just a street in that city, so I found three families I wanted to help, and went at it.

So, I bought myself a flat and started helping the carpenter's family, as they were helping with my windows and doors and they seemed like a good family to help. I learned a very, very hard lesson there. Throwing money at a problem isn't the solution. It doesn't take people out of poverty. All that happened was that I lost all my money, it was like throwing it into a well. You can give someone ten-thousand pounds to start a business, for example, but it doesn't work. The carpenter was going to open a mini-DIY shop, to sell door handles and hinges and that sort of thing. So, I gave him the money to buy stock, but then he ended up giving the money to his neighbour as his neighbour's wife needed an operation. I said you can't just do that, but he argued that he couldn't just let the wife die. It took me quite some time to work out that that's how it happens. They do just look after each other.

I really didn't understand how their culture worked, I just walked in there thinking I could fix poverty with money. Yes, money can help, but it's just fixing a small part of a problem. There's a saying that you can give a man a fish and he'd eat for a day. It was that saying, that made me think I do could much more if I encouraged people to start a business. I managed to help one family, whose son married and moved to the UK and started his own family. The downside of that, was that he doesn't send any money back home, which of course was the whole point of me helping. I eventually ran out of money, as you can imagine. I was there for around six years, and I went home with absolutely nothing. I just had my flight, that was it. I ended up having to explain to my mother that my own naivety had contributed to it.

When I look back now, having learned the ropes and the way the system worked, I can't believe that I was so naïve. There's just a magic in Egypt that doesn't exist anywhere else. I don't know whether it's because we grow up with all these images of the pyramids and ancient Egyptians, all the symbols, and learning all about this at school, but we just see this as an amazing, colourful, interesting place. It's also a history that we can visit, because it's still there and it feels authentic. You romanticize it, let's be honest. I'd romanticized it to the point where I could see the rubbish in the street, and their huge lack of cleanliness in their surroundings, but I still managed to look the other way.

CHARLIE – THAILAND

We met at a networking event, this regular meet up that happens in Bangkok on the third Thursday of every month. I rarely go, as I always find face to face networking a little weird and awkward, but my company sponsored this one and I thought I better show up. I was just in the corner, smashing the free wine and getting drunk, when she walked in. We then met for lunch a few days later, and we've been a couple since.

We got engaged on Christmas Day in Bali, and it was amazing. I paid for someone to set up flowers on the beach, to make it all look nice for when I proposed. It looked beautiful and she said yes, so from my point of view it went really well. I'd previously spoken to her Mum about the idea and she thought it was great. She said she was happy that I'd be joining her family, too. At that stage, it couldn't have gone any better. Once we got back to Thailand, we started talking about the wedding and coming up with plans. I really wanted to get married back at the same venue in Bali, as I thought it would be an amazing wedding location. It's the perfect place, as you can have the ceremony in this beautiful conservatory with the AC turned on, and then have the photos in the gardens. It helped that it was relatively cheap, about eight thousand in total, whereas you'd pay that for the venue alone in Thailand. So, I took some photos and showed her Mum, thinking that she'd love it. I hadn't expected her response, I'll be honest.

The first thing she said was, 'So who's paying for me to get there?' It took me back a little, but I said if it meant that much then I'd pay for her. Then she goes, 'Who's paying for the rest of the family, too?' By that stage, it was getting a little awkward. We talked it through as a couple and agreed that we'd pay for the flights for her immediate family, but they'd have to pay for the hotel. Seemed like a fair deal to me. Unfortunately, her Mum then wanted someone to pay for the hotel, too. It was getting stupid. The thing is her family are fairly well off. Her Mum owns land, she's got a business, she owns her house outright, she's not exactly struggling. She's got four kids, and she bought them all brand new cars on their eighteenth birthday. So, she can definitely afford her own flights to Bali. I'll be honest, I was finding it all a little sad and frustrating.

Anyway, we did get to the bottom of it, not that it's improved the situation. Basically, in Thailand you have to pay a dowry to get married. The man is seen as both responsible for the wedding and must gift a certain amount of money, gold, and jewelry to the family of the bride. Now, it turns out that if we got married in Bali, it wouldn't be considered a Thai ceremony. So, there'd be no envelopes of money, there'd be no cash or gold on plates that you can show off to your friends, none of that. Once I'd established this, we talked about the actual cost of the marriage. She directly asked me for one million baht, which is effectively twenty-five thousand pounds, to marry her daughter. As much as I love her, that's really ridiculous. I tried explaining that this wasn't how it worked in British culture, but that I was willing to meet her halfway, pay for the wedding, and pay to fly everyone out there, but I wasn't going to give her twenty-five grand on top of that.

The problem is, they don't have pension plans and the like here. So, they use their daughters as their retirement or their nest egg, and they think that sets them up for life. The way they calculate the dowry is then based on a few factors. If she's from a very rich family, then the price is high, if she's a virgin it's higher, if they haven't been married before, and all sorts of things like that. I said, you know, I don't feel like we should negotiate over how much a person is worth, they aren't a piece of meat, we haven't gone down to the market here to buy a cow. Then I really pissed my fiancé off as I said she's not under thirty, she's not from a rich family, she's not a virgin, and she's been married before. So, with that in mind, I don't see why I should pay as much. So, that was the wrong move as I'd now pissed everyone off.

The whole thing, it's just turned into a massive nightmare, mate. We were really looking forward to it all, but now it's turned into this huge clusterfuck of stress and negativity, and it's really soured it all. However, everyone I've spoken to in Thailand has said the same. It's really shit. It makes getting married here stressful.

DEALING WITH DISAPPOINTMENT

OLIVIA – PANAMA & COLOMBIA

Being back in London right now, staying at my brother's place, really wasn't how I saw this going. At the time I came home, I was sailing from Colombia to Panama and making my way to the San Blas Islands. I was working but I wasn't getting paid, almost a trial for getting a paid job working on the boats out there. When we left from Colombia to Panama, there was thirty hours of open sea and we couldn't talk to anyone or hear anything. By the time we got there, the pandemic had escalated, and we were told that the passengers had to leave the boats immediately and that we weren't allowed to leave the island. There was so much bullshit going on, though. I was just watching and listening to the news. People were saying airports were going to close, that this was going to close, all sorts. The military came over to the boat and said we all had to stay there for six weeks. It's crazy how paradise can turn into something so terrifying when you want to leave but you can't. I remember looking at these islands and thinking, 'Oh man, I don't want to be here.' I just completely panicked. Fortunately, my Dad's friend has a hotel in Panama, and I stayed there for a week, and then eventually got home.

Before leaving for Colombia, I used to work for charities in victim support. It's mostly around domestic and sexual violence, so it was often alongside the police, and it was all very heavy work. Despite being passionate about these issues, I would still get frustrated and I noticed how I started to care less about what I was dealing with. I think that was just my way of trying to cope with the reality of it all. Supposedly that's quite common, that you try to find a way to blame the victim in these situations to balance your views of the world. By that, I mean that you think bad things happen to bad people, good things happen to good people. When you see bad things happening to good people, it starts to mess with how you view the world. After a while in that environment, you really do need a break.

I had a contract for a year, and I was always under the impression that it would get renewed, but there ended up being funding delays for around six months. So, given that enforced break, I decided I'd go off and try to learn Spanish somewhere. I'd ideally like to move to Spain at some point, but I also really like South America and thought I'd give that a try first. So, I went out to visit a friend who was doing circus training out in Colombia for a holiday and fell in love with the place. When I got back to England, I had what was far beyond holiday blues. I couldn't believe that I voluntarily stayed in this country and that I wasn't getting out and seeing other places. So, off the hoof, I decided to book a flight to Colombia later in the year. I didn't really have a plan or an idea of what I'd be doing, but just knew I wanted to go back there. I ended up getting a recommendation from a friend about a language school in Medellin and booked myself into that to start with. That led to me meeting a few people and going off traveling for a bit, including as a passenger to the San Blas Islands. I realised then that I wanted to actually work, rather than just keep traveling. Obviously, you know what happened then, the pandemic hit, and I made the decision to come home.

Colombia is always associated with Pablo Escobar, but what you see in the tv shows is far from the reality of living there. The older generation, the ones that lived through it, they absolutely hate him. They hate that there's sightseeing tours around his house and that you can visit the filming locations for the Netflix series. In general, they're very sensitive to any talk of cocaine and violence. Supposedly in the '80s, it was one of the deadliest places in the world. Whereas today? Not really, but you do have to keep your wits about you and be switched on. Unfortunately, I learned that the hard way. I was preaching to everyone about how safe it was, how completely at home I felt, and then I got mugged. I had a friend visiting and they said they wanted to go and paddle their feet in the sea before bed. We were sat having a cigarette when three men with knives turned up, pulled us apart, grabbed our earrings and our bags, including the keys to my apartment, and left.

I just completely panicked and felt out of my depth at that point. However, it was a real reality check for me. I saw what happened if you relaxed too much and dropped your guard. Fortunately, we got into the apartment, spent some time with the police, and I completely understood why it all happened. I ended up feeling sorry for the people who mugged us, as they didn't really get anything. My phone screen was cracked and then I got it blocked, the earrings weren't expensive, and there was hardly any cash in my bag. So, they're threatening people with knives and they didn't get much. They looked young and quite scared. I held onto my bag as I thought they'd get spooked and run away, but then it ended up being worse. They held me down and pulled my earrings out of my ears. It was fairly humbling, though, and I learned my lesson.

KATIE - GERMANY

Having lived in Germany before, as I'd spent time in both Berlin and Heidelberg while doing my degree, the idea to go back out and take my masters in Bonn just made so much sense. The course itself was very difficult to get into and I was naturally pretty excited when I found out that I'd got a place. It seemed like this huge opportunity and the chance to go back to a country that I absolutely loved, so what's not to get excited about? The problem was that it ended up not going the way I planned at all.

I moved out in the September and really loved the first few months. I was studying in Bonn and working part time at the Hard Rock Café in Cologne. Sure, that's quite a touristy place, but it was a job and one where I could still speak German when I needed to. When January came round though, my Nannan came to visit and while she was there, I got a phone call from my Dad to tell me that my other Nannan had been diagnosed with cancer. It was quite shocking and put living abroad into a different perspective for me. Everything I'd previously found cool and exciting about being there, that just disappeared in an instance. I started to question why I was away, why I hadn't just stayed at home, and why I had chosen to isolate myself from the rest of the family.

Unfortunately, those feelings deepened in the April that year. I was at a lake enjoying the sunshine with my friends and after getting out of the water, I tried to call my Granddad, who I called Gags. We used to regularly talk on the phone, me and Gags, and I remember him saying, 'Make sure you ring me when you're out of that lake,' as he used to worry about things like that. So as soon as I was out, I gave him a call. No-one answered at the time, though, so I carried on having a barbecue and trying to enjoy myself. Sadly, the worst thing in the world was happening at the time, as he'd had a massive heart attack and was dying. I didn't find out for a few hours though, due to all the chaos back home. I got the phone call at 1am. I remember just sitting there on my own thinking, 'Holy crap', and then having to grieve on my own. Everyone else was back home, all going through that same process together, and I was just sat here alone not knowing what to do. In that exact moment, I really wish I hadn't moved abroad and that I was back there with them all.

When someone you love dies and you're not there, and not around family or friends who knew the person, you really don't know what to do with yourself. I thought I'd just get a flight that day, but life really doesn't work like that. You have to put stuff in place, tell your work, make arrangements. I remember telling my supervisor that I wanted to take a week off, but she was very unsympathetic about it and asked why I couldn't just go for the day and be back at work as soon as possible. I really couldn't do that, though. My Granddad meant the world to me, he was one of my favourite people, he was always so funny and full of life. His death came as a real surprise to everyone. He was doing fine, so we just didn't see it coming. Obviously, as they're older than you, your grandparents are often the first people you see die, but it doesn't make that any easier for you. To see that unfold remotely, when you're the only one from your family not there, that's really hard.

When you live abroad, everyone seems to naturally assume that you're fine. 'Oh, Katie's fine, she's living in Germany,' they'll say. I really wasn't fine, but it seemed hard to tell people that. They often have this idea that you're this incredibly independent person, that you've made this choice to be away from everyone, and can always deal with anything thrown at you. In reality, I was struggling. I'd previously based my whole personality around Germany and being comfortable in that country, yet I could no longer enjoy any of it. It was such a formative experience to go through, that disconnect from everyone and everything around me. Dealing with the worst thing that's ever happened and doing that on my own, that was really difficult. I had the extreme highs of getting to achieve my dreams and study in Germany, combined with the extreme low of the death and ill-health of those I loved. In those moments, living away seemed like a selfish pursuit, even though I knew it was what I wanted and what my life had been leading up to for so long. It was hard.

VICKY – SWEDEN, AUSTRIA, & GERMANY

I suffer from hearing loss and because I wear hearing aids, I was always told that I'd struggle with languages. However, whenever someone tells me I can't do something or I'll find something hard, I just think, 'Well screw them,' and it makes me want to do something more. So, I studied German at school, then went on to read business with German at university, partly based on the idea that I was told I'd struggle. With my degree, I spent a year in Munich working for a German company. I'll be honest and say that I was working in English and my friendship group were mostly English, but it was still a great first experience outside of the UK for me. The work itself was a bit bland, as it was just a regular internship, but the lifestyle there was awesome. We'd work during the day and then head out in the evenings, mostly to drink or to party. I was devastated to leave at the end of it, absolutely devastated. I went there as this young, slightly nervous girl and it just gave me so much confidence in myself.

While in Munich, I learned to ski. It's a city that's really close to the mountains, either in Germany or in Austria, so we did a few trips down there over that winter. Skiing and snowboarding weren't something that my family had ever done, and it's not something you can easily do in England, so this was my first experience. I absolutely loved it though, and while there I got talking to the staff about how I'd get a job there in Austria for a season. It gave me something to do after university for a bit, and that first winter after graduating, I did my first ski season. I was on breakfast duty, but it was still an amazing experience. You've got the mountain air, you wake up every day, look outside and you've got these snowy mountains and that feeling of freedom. It was immense. You had to work, sure, but that was just part of life there. Everyone there was working in a bar, or cleaning, or cooking, and everyone just accepted it and got on with it. There was a lot of parties, a lot of good times there, and you really felt like you were in a bubble. I ended up doing three seasons there, too.

From working those ski seasons, I'd meet a lot of Scandinavians, a lot of Danes, a lot of Swedes. In fact, I'd started picking up a bit of Swedish from them as a result. And that gave me this idea. I didn't really want to go back to the UK and get into a normal, full time job if I'm totally honest. So, what if I just moved to Sweden instead and give that a go? I did go home in between that, just to save up some money, and then I moved to Stockholm. I ended up only spending two months there, as I tried but ultimately failed to find a job. It was a great experience, but my money started to run out quickly and I was getting absolutely nowhere with my job search. I gave my C.V to hundreds of people, but no one would ever respond, and eventually I had to call time on it. At the time, I felt like I massively failed in Sweden. The problem was, I didn't really have a plan for my life then, and I definitely wasn't able to find one in Sweden, either. I might've given up on the idea too soon, but I didn't want to be begging my Mum for money.

I wouldn't go anywhere nowadays without a plan, probably because I have more to lose, but I'm still proud of myself for trying Germany, Austria, and even Sweden. I was young and it didn't all work out for me, but what did I really lose? Just living in these countries, it gave me a real buzz and this real sense of achievement. When you live in a different country and you're away from your nearest and dearest, it's not always going to be easy, is it? I think it teaches you to step out of your comfort zone, though. It's very easy to get wrapped up in your own world if you don't travel or experience new cultures. Then you do it, it's like opening a new book you've never read before. You find so much that you didn't previously know, both about yourself and about the world in general. Just experiencing that, you really do grow as a person. I learned a hell of a lot about myself during those years. I think the experience I gained is absolutely priceless now. I don't think I'll ever regret it.

CHLOE – FRANCE & SPAIN

I'd always loved learning to speak French, as had my Mum, and I had it in my head from an early age that I'd move to France one day. That fascination with languages and other cultures stayed with me throughout, leading to me studying French and Spanish languages and translation at university. The course was ideal for me, too, as it gave me the chance of living in both countries during my year abroad. Having previously spent time in Normandy, where I'd regularly get the boat across and stay with good friends, I was far more excited about the French half of the year. In the end though, the time in Spain was far better and it's why I'm living back there now. I was up in Northern Spain, somewhere tourists rarely go, and I enjoyed it far more than I expected. What I wasn't expecting, was how miserable I'd find my time back in France after that.

I was studying in Angers, a town on the Loire Valley, and I ended up hating every single second of it. While it's a small but beautiful place, it has absolutely no atmosphere and no sense of unity. The French locals didn't want to know us students at all, despite the fact we were speaking the language and spending money in the community, and we just never felt welcomed. I know that the French and English do have a certain animosity with each other at times, but it really took me by surprise. We weren't the only ones who weren't welcome, either. There were clear divisions between the locals and the immigrants, especially the Muslim and Eastern European residents. You could see these distinct communities there, and a general sense of unrest and resentment hung in the air the whole time.

It wasn't just Angers, either. We took a trip to Nantes to visit my friend and unfortunately got caught up in protests there. When we arrived on the train, we noticed all these police vans lining the street. Clearly something was up, but the Tourist Info assured us that there was nothing to worry about and encouraged us to just continue our day. So, we carried on and my friend took the chance to go up a tower, this typically tourist place, just to see the views. She came down soon after to tell us that she could see a stand-off nearby between the police with their water cannons on one side, and protestors setting fire to things and throwing objects on the other. It suddenly felt very unsafe and very volatile, so we just wanted to get out of there. The further we went, the more vandalism, smashed windows, and even cars on fire that we saw. It really felt like we were in a warzone, even more so when others started running towards us and people started throwing petrol bombs at the advancing police. It was terrifying.

Perhaps it was naïve of me, but my six months in Angers completely ruined my illusion of life in France. If anything, I felt really deceived by it all. It was nothing like Normandy, which always felt very welcoming, and it made me really take a step back and view the country differently. Maybe I'll try going there on holiday again, but I can't see myself ever living in the country again.

HEADING HOME

KYLIE – USA

I met an American while I was on holiday in Jamaica and that really changed the direction of my life. At first my friends and family were pretty shocked by it, but we started video chatting the minute I got back from that holiday. So, when the time came to meet him in person, they'd already spoken to him through these video calls and they could see that he wasn't catfishing me. It was almost like they'd known him for years when he first came to the UK. We were only together for a week after our wedding, and then he went back to Iowa while I was waiting for my visa to be processed. In a way, it wasn't any different to what we were used to. We'd had two years of the long distance between us, and this just felt like a continuation of that. We were legally married and had that official label, but nothing really changed. We did see each other, and we'd visit throughout, but applying for that visa and being able to live in America with him was a long, long process.

Before moving to Iowa, I'd never really been anywhere like it. It's mainly pig farming here, in fact there's comfortably more pigs than people in this state. It takes six hours to drive from one side to the other, too, so it's just miles of flat, pig farming land. Back home, I was used to living in a decent sized town in Essex, with easy trips into London whenever I wanted them. Whereas here, I'm now in a town of about three thousand people and it's a good three hours away from a big city like Des Moines or Chicago. It does mean there's no traffic here, that and the cost of living being far more affordable, but it can feel pretty isolating when you're not used to it. The weather can swing between really hot in the summer, to absolutely freezing in the winter, too. The school I'm working in now, that closed last year because it was minus fifty degrees at one stage. Okay, that's way below the average, which is normally around minus ten or so, but let me tell you, that's ridiculously cold.

With Iowans, even though we're speaking the same language, the mentality can be very different. They've very laid-back here, yet when it comes to things like owning a gun, they're suddenly all for it. They'll often say, 'I'm not going to shoot anyone, so why can't I have a gun?' I don't think they see it as carrying this weapon of death around with them. They just argue that it's their right, that they have a right to carry one if they want. There's also this funny story about how a speed camera an hour from me was removed as too many people were complaining about it infringing on their rights. Apparently, they have a right to face their persecutor, rather than being caught by a camera. There's this belief that if it's not a human catching you, they aren't willing to accept it. I can find these arguments really hard to get my head around, but that's part of living somewhere else, you just have to deal with it.

I always felt a pressure to move away from home, but I didn't imagine it would be to Iowa. I've struggled with that at times, too. I think in life, you often go through milestones at a decent pace. You know, you pass your driving test at seventeen, you get your first proper job, you meet someone, you move in together, you get married, etc. Whereas I was experiencing everything at the same time. I was suddenly a wife, I was living in a new country, working in a new job, sleeping in a new bed, re-taking my driving test again. It was all happening to me in one go, rather than paced out. It felt a little overwhelming at times, but I did learn to adapt to it and get through it all. What helped, was writing my own blog and then publishing my own book. I started by documenting my visa process, writing down my feelings, explaining how I was finding it. I felt like I need to unbottle these thoughts and find a way to release them. If I'm honest, I never thought I'd release a book, but it's really helped.

Despite learning to adapt out here, I've realized that I don't see myself living here for much longer. I'd like to be back in England, that's where I'd like to be. I'd always made it clear to my husband that I didn't see myself dying in Iowa, but I was willing to give America a try. We had those discussions when we spoke about me moving out here, knowing that it might become a problem for me. I've always found it a struggle, though. I miss my family, I miss the coast, I miss going down to places like Clacton and Southend whenever I want to. For me, being by the coast is my happy place, yet I'm now one thousand miles from it, and even then, it's a lake. The problem is, I moved to be with a person, not to be in a particular place. I'd love to be closer to a city again, to have other British people around me, to really feel like I'm at home again. Iowa isn't that, no matter how much I try to make this my home.

Moving here was just one of those things. What if I didn't move and hadn't given this a chance? What if I was missing out on the best life I could have? Without taking that leap, and going with some hope and some trust, I just would never know. The thing is, I've been a huge traveller since I was sixteen, but I always got to go home at the end of that. I think it's time that I go home now, too.

RYAN – UNITED ARAB EMIRATES

I was working for a well-known company back in Leeds, managing teams who look after customers, when I was approached by someone on LinkedIn asking if I'd ever considered working in Dubai. I hadn't, mate, as I'm sure most people haven't. I was sceptical at first, so asked for the job description and did a bit of a background check on the guy, just to be sure. It all looked real though, and most of the information was pretty easy to find online. I also checked out Dubai a bit and found out that they had tax free earnings, which sounded pretty decent to me. So, I said I was interested, had a telephone interview, sent them across a few bits of proof, and was offered the job after a video interview with the guy who is now my boss. The process was very, very quick, it was around three months from being contacted, to starting my new job in Dubai.

Because it all happened so quickly, I didn't really take stock of what was happening, as strange as that may sound. From having the interviews, being offered the job, and then having to make plans to leave Leeds, it just flew by. It meant I never just sat down and thought about how I was feeling. I was more concerned with getting everything in order, that my partner was doing alright, that sort of thing. It didn't help that I was busy at work, doing ten, twelve hour shifts at the same time as trying to organize this big move. In between all that, we had a two-week holiday to Florida booked. I figured I wasn't cancelling that as it gave me quality time with my fiancé, and possibly the last time for a while, and I wasn't missing that. I guess I saw it as this great opportunity, a bit of a steppingstone to a more senior role back home, and maybe a chance to make a bit of money. But really, it was so quick, that I just ran with it.

When I was going through the recruitment process, none of it was common knowledge among my friends and family. In all elements of my life, I tend to only speak to people once things are confirmed. I never really want to jinx something or add that extra complication to the mix. I felt like I needed to get my head around the idea first and make the right decision for myself. Of course, I'd told my fiancé and she was fully aware, but we kept it to ourselves while I was being interviewed. I'd be lying if I said that wasn't stressful, though. The idea of uprooting myself, moving to what felt like the other side of the world, that was definitely a bit of a challenge for me. Once it was confirmed, I did start telling people and fortunately they were all really supportive. Some of the elderly family members worried that they wouldn't see much of me, but hopefully they understood that it was this great opportunity.

Before moving here, I'd never been to the Middle East before. I had no idea about Dubai as a country, didn't know the culture, nothing like that. The company were great, though, and really helped me ease in. I was welcomed at the airport by a guy holding a sign with my name on it, which I'd never had before, and he rushed me through immigration, sorted my visa, and then took me to the hotel I stayed in while looking for my own place. I had my fiancé with me for that first month, which massively helped, and it was great to have her support. The thing is though, I flew on the Friday and then started working on the Sunday, as the working week is Sunday to Thursday here. So, we flew in, went to the supermarket, had the Saturday free, and then started working on the Sunday. It was all very quick. And since then, I've been working pretty long hours, maybe seventy hours a week at times. It probably sounds boring, doesn't it? But it's fine for me. I came here to work hard, to earn some money, and get this new experience. Sure, I can look out and see the amazing sights here, but I've had very little time to do that if I'm honest.

From a cultural perspective, everything is based around what people perceive as lavish and luxurious, and it's probably easy to get caught up in that. For me, it's been a massive change, but

I've managed to say fairly humble and keep in line with what I'd do in England. I cook for myself; I clean for myself; I work hard, I don't buy anything I wouldn't do back home. Don't get me wrong, I'd love to walk into one of these car showrooms and look at some Lamborghinis or Ferraris, but I'm not realistically going to buy one of those, am I? It's certainly a far cry from Leeds on a Saturday, though.

I probably sound like a boring, sensible guy from Leeds, but that's exactly what I am. I'm grateful for this opportunity and I don't regret it for a second, but there are times when I miss home. I miss Leeds, I do. It might sound strange, but there's a local pub called the Tommy Wass there, and I lived a stone's throw from it. I was a ten-minute walk from Elland Road, too. I used just go into the pub after work, have a chat to some lads, go down the football at the weekend. It was good, and I guess I never considered leaving that before this came up. I said to people here that I'd see out my three-year visa and then back to the UK, but apparently that's what everyone says and then they never leave. Let's see, hey?

JAMES – USA

I was figuring it all out for a while. I knew I could give teaching a go, having worked with children with the Scouts and again at a summer camp in Florida, but I took a few temp jobs in between to save some money. I worked in a Starbucks for a few months. I got a job as an admin at a software company. Then, I got some work experience at a school. And after that, it was some more admin work for the NHS. So, there were definitely a few years where I was trying to work out what I wanted to do. After I did my teacher training in Cambridge though, it did all start falling together. I ended up doing a masters there, teaching for a while, and then moved down to London to work in a private school there.

I had a few friends in Cambridge who'd gone abroad, so the idea of doing similar had been kicking around in my head for a while. I was living with my girlfriend at the time, she's also a teacher, and we decided we could give that a go. I applied for a role in Singapore but didn't get that far with that. Then we both applied for jobs in Chicago. She got really far with that, but I was eliminated quite early, so I just started looking for other opportunities. I saw one in California, which obviously sounded great, and just sent off an email without really thinking much more. Anyway, later that week I got an interview, and was eventually offered it after a bit of a wait. So, there was a period where she was waiting to hear back from the job in Chicago, and I was sat waiting to hear back about one in Palo Alto. There was always that thought at the back of my mind, the what if we end up in different cities? As it turned out, she wasn't offered her role, but I got mine. We then decided to get married quickly so she could come with me, largely for the sake of the visa.

I think, deep down, I really wanted to go anyway. It had always been a dream to live longer term in another country, rather than just doing some extended travel, and to gain that experience of setting myself up somewhere else. I wanted to try being away, being somewhere permanently, rather than just a year traveling. Despite its faults, I've always really enjoyed working in America. I've always had a great time over here, and there's just something about this place that I'd always liked. I'd never been to Palo Alto before, but I had been to San Francisco, up to Fresno, down to Los Angeles, and San Diego, but just not this exact area. I did worry that it would be super expensive, and in fact the person they originally offered the role to had pulled out because they worried the area was too expensive. It's nuts here, it's absolutely insane. At first, when I moved here, I tried to find a cheaper place and wanted to save some money. Then, once you get here, you don't want to live far from work and in some shit hole out in the middle of nowhere, so you just end up paying more.

In general, once you get over the crazy costs here, then you can enjoy it. I've been here for three years now and I think living in this area, that's been the best part of the experience. You can drive to the beach, you can drive to Yosemite, you can go skiing in the mountains, you can go to the forest, you can drive to the desert. You can drive to so much within a day. The nature in this area is incredible and that was what wowed me at first. I've never lived in an area with this much diversity before. The hiking, the scenery, the nature. It's amazing.

As for working in the school, that's been fine and I've enjoyed it, but unfortunately it looks like my time here is coming to an end. My stay has always been a little temporary because of my visa situation, but it looks like the school now aren't willing to risk being without a teacher at short notice if, for whatever reason, my visa isn't renewed. It's the same for my wife, too. I think we've been a little unlucky with the timing, though. The school previously had visa issues with other members of staff, so they're probably just done with the whole situation. It wouldn't surprise me if they were just replacing us with Americans to guarantee they'll have teachers, either. I do see their point, too, but I feel like they could've tried a little harder. It's a real shame and I wish it wasn't ending like this, but I guess this time it's my turn to leave.

For me, I think I'll head back to London, go back to the school that I used to work at, and just enjoy being back in London for a while. There are plenty of other international teaching jobs going, and I could get definitely one, but I don't think I'll go somewhere else just for the sake of it. Going somewhere just to be abroad? No, I don't so. I think the value I've learned here is the importance of having friends and family nearby. I've missed just going down the pub with a mate after work or seeing my Mum and sister regularly. I'll probably change my mind in the grey January weather in London, won't I? My wife and I aren't sure what the future holds for us, though. There have been some strains on the relationship, and we've drifted apart a little, so we might not be going back home as a couple. Will we both end up in London and living in the same place? I'm not so sure.

I feel like life is in chapters, and this is just one chapter coming to an end. This has been great, I've had an awesome time, and I really hope the next chapter, and the one after, will be just as good. I wish I could stay here, but it's not to be this time.

JOE – UKRAINE & VIETNAM

I didn't really know what I wanted to do with my life back then. I'd got my master's degree, had applied to university to study for a PhD but hadn't heard back, and I'd also done some traveling in Eastern Europe for a few months. But what I was doing next, I wasn't sure. I didn't really want to start a career as such, so I was just working in Wetherspoons while I worked it all out. What changed for me, was breaking up with my girlfriend. It made me want to get away for a bit and, to be honest, just change my life plans and try something new. As I had a friend living out in Vietnam, and I'd always wanted to visit Asia, I decided I'd head out there for a year or so. The plan was to do some traveling and hopefully pick up a few jobs teaching English, just to give me some money to live on.

I started out in Thailand and did a bit of traveling there, before moving on to Vietnam a month later. That first night I arrived in Hanoi, that was pretty eye-opening. It was dark, I was in a new country, and I didn't have a working phone, so I just jumped on the bus and hoped to find the right address. The roads were outrageously busy, though, so I had this real trepidation for even something as simple as crossing the street.

You've got thousands of scooters and motorbikes beeping at you, cars swerving pedestrians, and you just have to step out into the street and trust that you'll be fine. Once you learn the system though, it all makes sense. Within a few months, I realised that I couldn't just use my English driving style out there and expect it to work. You learn that you're just responsible for avoiding what's in front of you. You've also got a pecking order, so bikes move for cars, cars move for trucks, and that's the pecking order. It's pretty fascinating to see and everyone seems fine with it, too.

I'd arrived in Vietnam with a lot less money than I'd hoped to have, so ended up staying on a mate's floor at the beginning. I didn't really enjoy it at first, if I'm honest. I felt completely out of my depth, too. It turns out I was experiencing a bit of culture shock; I just didn't realise it at the time. I was out of cash, trying to settle into the country, trying to make it all work. It was all happening at the same time, so it felt a little daunting to me. If anything, it did force me to adapt quickly, though. I eventually earned enough to move into a spare room at my mate's apartment, and from there I could start enjoying that quote unquote ex-pat life. You have relatively little responsibility, a big group of people around you, and that can be a lot of fun. Hanoi has a huge international community, so you'll find lots of British, Irish, and South Africans living out there. They'll mostly be traveling, working in tourism, or teaching English as a foreign language. People use teaching to fund their traveling, so they'll go somewhere for a month, teach, and then move onto the next country. It does mean that there's a high turnover of staff, though, which helped me pick up some cover lessons and find extra work.

While I was out there, I got a reply from university to say that I could start my PhD in September, which was great news. What had changed though, was that I'd met a Ukrainian girl and had fallen for her. With me going back to England to study, and her moving on to Thailand, I just assumed that would be the end of the relationship and we'd go our separate ways. It was disappointing, of course, but it just seemed a natural ending. However, after a few months apart, neither of us wanted to do that. So, we started looking for ways we could stay together. With Ukraine not being part of the EU or the ECC, it made getting a UK visa for her extremely difficult. She either needed to have a job with a thirty-thousand pound starting salary, be studying for a degree, or have a family member who was earning at least eighteen-thousand six-hundred pounds a year to cover for her. None of those were an option for us, though. I'd been out of the country and didn't meet that earning threshold, and she didn't have a job to move into or a degree to study for. We also had some added complications with her birth certificate and passport, which didn't help. So, it was all proving very, very difficult. I didn't want to split up from this girl, though, so we eventually moved to Ukraine and got married out here.

I'm now studying for my PhD remotely, which the university allowed, and I've been teaching English out here to make money. It's a funny one, though. Had you asked me a year ago whether I wanted to be here or in the UK, I'd have one-hundred percent said the UK. No doubt about it. But now? I honestly don't know. I'd love to live closer to friends and family, but I didn't want to lose this relationship to do that. I feel a little resentful because of the situation and how difficult I've found it, if I'm honest. I'm genuinely very happy out here, though. The people are friendly, it's cheap to live, and I'm enjoying my work. I'm not sure if we'll stay here forever, but it's working for now.

TRACEY – USA

I left school when I was seventeen years old, halfway through my A Levels. I decided I couldn't stand it there anymore, and as my father ran a famous equestrian centre in Somerset, I was able to leave and focus my time on horses instead. I was fortunate, in that sense. That background in horses allowed me to travel and work in France, in New Zealand, and eventually across here in North America.

I first came to America when I was twenty-three years old, initially to train with a professional horse rider. We were based in this horse-riding centre in Maryland, but then spent thirty-six weeks of the year on the road. We'd be in Florida, then Toronto, then in Arizona, then Detroit, we'd even do shows at Madison Square Gardens in New York. It was an exciting lifestyle and I really got to see how varied the geography of the country was. I also soon realised that most places had the same stores, the same strip malls, and they were all laid out in the same way, with the same products. Their location just changed, that's all. I only intended to stay for six months; I'd never planned to live full-time here. I didn't feel much of a connection to the country. I thought it was too fast, too brash, too money-orientated, and too violent. In fact, it felt very violent to me. I was there for the experience, but I thought I'd go back to Somerset at the end of the six months. To find myself here thirty years later, having raised two children here? I'd have laughed at you back then if you told me that.

I met a guy, though. I met this charming American, who was in the US Navy and working as a chemical and nuclear engineer, and that changed it all for me. We got married in England and our intentions were to live in the UK. That's where my soul has always been and where my emotional state has always felt most comfortable. However, the job prospects in my husband's field were stronger in the U.S, so we stuck around, had children, and just never found our way back. Before you know it, you're into twenty-five, thirty years of living somewhere and wondering where it all went. If you'd told me on my wedding day that I was signing up for another thirty years here, I'd have probably bolted. Obviously, part of my heart was connected to my husband, and that's where I found myself torn over the years.

My husband is from California, and we met and lived in Connecticut, so I always say that we travelled three-thousand miles each and met in the middle. We moved to California after a year and ended up living in a place called Victorville. It's effectively a truck stop on your way to Las Vegas. I hated it there, but he needed to be there for his work. Four years, ten months, three weeks, and two days. That's how long we lived there. It felt like I'd landed on the moon. I was honestly counting the days until we could leave. I just found people there to be very materialistic. It was all about how many cars you had, what your house looked like, what nice things you could afford. It was quite miserable, really. When my husband was eventually offered a job in New England, I knew I could do that. I was delighted to move back to somewhere with smaller towns, beautiful village greens, older buildings. It just had much more of a comfortable vibe and I really needed that closer familiarity to my homeland.

With my husband traveling for work, and my last child leaving for colleague, I eventually found myself sitting at home on my own frequently. I was a speech-language pathologist by trade, so worked in hospitals and schools. I loved the students and patients but found the work environments too stressful. I quit my job and started writing and exploring my thoughts about England as a result. That's where my first book, 'Dunster's Calling', came from. Its fiction but based on my own mission to try to get home. There's this Celtic word, hiraeth, which translates as an intense yearning for home, a longing for a place that may no longer exists. I based my first book on that feeling, and a lot of people who've read the book felt like they could relate to it, too. They knew they were longing for something else but had never been able to put their finger on it. They were also not clear whether that something else would still be there for them when they got home. And I've always wondered that, too. Am I looking for a scene or a view that just reminds me of my early years? Does that even still exist?

After thirty years in America, I'm about to find out. With no reason to be tied to this country anymore, as we no longer have a mortgage or children dependent on us, we finally felt like we could move to the place we felt happiest. That was always going to be England for me. My soul has been yearning to return there ever since I first stepped foot in America. There's something about Exmoor in particular, where I'll be moving to, that helps me sleep my best and breathe the deepest. I've always felt incredibly relaxed and at home there. I've been trying to explore that feeling for years and have yet to find anything that fully explains it. I hope I finally have the one-way ticket I've been looking for.

A ROUND OF APPLAUSE

The following people deserve a round of applause for their contributions to this book:

Craig Taylor, for inspiring me with his own book, 'Londoners'. Tom Fay who, while hiking together in Osaka, convinced me this was an idea worth pursuing. My Mum, Sally, for her unwavering belief that my words make good reading. It's just a shame that Nanny isn't here to read them now, hey Mum? John Davis and Adam Nuttall for their solid feedback and suggestions. MJ, Janet, Belinda, Rebecca, Kylie, Gary, Ryan, Tracey, and Amanda for their words of encouragement at times when I needed them most. Dan Bazeley, Jamie Barker, and Vicki Willis for being the first readers out in the wild. Sophie Lauren Smith for the excellent cover design and for bringing my ideas to life. And last, but certainly not least, Yvonne for not only her proof-reading, but also for accepting the hours I spent in the spare room talking to 'strangers' while researching this book. They don't feel like strangers anymore, that's for sure.

Thank you for reading this far. As a first-time, independent author, I rely heavily on word of mouth recommendations and sharing. So, if you've enjoyed this book, it would be great if you could tell your family, friends, or online contacts about it. If you'd like free digital copies to share with them, whether e-pub or PDF files, send me a message and I'll happily help. While financial rewards are welcome, I care more about my work being read by as many people as possible.

If you're a British citizen who lives or has lived outside of Britain and would like to be featured in a future version of this book, I'd also love to hear from you.

For more information and contact details, visit:

GoodbyeBritain.co.uk

Printed in Great Britain
by Amazon

57757684R00129